P9-EEK-945

MACMILLAN
MUSIC and YOU

Cover Design and Illustration
Heather Cooper

Illustration Credits
Marilyn Bass
Marilyn Janovitz
Robert LoGrippo
Steve Madson
Jan Pyk
Bob Shein
Jerry Smath
Joel Snyder
Richard Steadham
Mou-Sien Tseng
Sally Vitsky
Lane Yerkes

MACMILLAN
MUSIC and YOU

Barbara Staton, Senior Author
Merrill Staton, Senior Author
Marilyn Davidson
Phyllis Kaplan
Susan Snyder

Macmillan Publishing Company

New York

Collier Macmillan Publishers

London

ACKNOWLEDGMENTS

Grateful acknowledgment is given to the following authors and publishers. In the case of songs and poems for which acknowledgment is not given, we have earnestly endeavored to find the original source and to procure permission for their use, but without success. Extensive research failed to locate the author and/or copyright holder.

A. LEDUC & Cie for *Hani Kouni* from LAMELOU by Jos Wuytack. Reprinted by permission of A. LEDUC & Cie.

Alfred Publishing Co. for *Aardvarks on the Ark* by Mary Val Marsh. Copyright © 1978 by Alfred Publishing Co. International Copyright Secured. Made in U.S.A. All rights reserved.

Augsburg Publishing House for *Many in One* by Alice Parker. Copyright © 1987 Augsburg Publishing House. Used by permission.

Birch Tree Group Ltd. for *Sit on the Green Grass* by Patti Schliestett from the JOY OF MUSIC. Copyright © 1967 Birch Tree Group Ltd. All rights reserved. Used by permission.

Boosey & Hawkes for *Ching-a-ring Chaw* by Aaron Copland from OLD AMERICAN SONGS. Copyright © 1954 by Aaron Copland; Copyright Renewed. Boosey & Hawkes, Inc., Sole Publisher and Licensee. Reprinted by permission.

Oscar Brand for *I'se the B'y*, a folk song from Newfoundland from SINGING HOLIDAYS, Knopf 1957. Copyright © 1957 by Oscar Brand. Reprinted by his permission.

Canadian Museum of Civilization for *Lots o' Fish in Bonavist' Harbor*, from FOLKSONGS FROM NEWFOUNDLAND, collected by Stephen Peacock. Reprinted courtesy of the Canadian Museum of Civilization.

Wayne Chadwick for the musical *Pets* © 1986 by Wayne Chadwick. Used by permission.

Cherry Lane Music Publishing Co., Inc. for *Going Camping* by Ray Charles. Copyright © 1983 Cherry Lane Music Publishing Co., Inc./Cherry Mountain Music/Muppet Music, Inc.; *Grandma's Feather Bed* by Jim Connor. Copyright © 1973 Cherry River Music Co. All Rights Reserved. Used by permission.

Crown Publishers for *Open the Window, Noah*, reprinted from AMERICAN NEGRO SONGS & SPIRITUALS by John W. Work. Copyright © 1968 by Crown Publishers, Inc. Used by permission of Crown Publishers, Inc.

Randy DeLelles and Jeff Kriske for *The Stonecutter*. Used by permission.

Doubleday & Company, Inc. for *Eagle Flight* and *I Go Forth to Move About the Earth* by Alonzo Lopez from THE WHISPERING WIND edited by Terry Allen. Copyright © 1972 by Institute of American Indian Arts. Reprinted by permission of Doubleday & Company, Inc.

Farrar, Straus & Giroux, Inc. for *Harvest* (also titled *Harvest Time*) adapted from SLAVE SONGS OF THE GEORGIA SEA ISLANDS by Lydia Parrish. Copyright 1942 by Lydia Parrish, copyright renewed © 1969 by Maxfield Parrish, Jr. Reprinted by permission of Farrar, Straus & Giroux, Inc.

Biff P. Fink III for *Hoopster*. Copyright © 1982 by Biff Fink. Pamela W. Haft for the Orff Orchestration of *Ahrirang*. Reprinted by permission of Pamela W. Haft.

Hap-Pal Music for *The Eagle* by Hap Palmer and Martha Palmer from HAP PALMER FAVORITES. Used by permission of the Publisher, Alfred Publishing.

Margaret Hillert for *Farther Than Far*. Copyright © 1969; *And Suddenly Spring* from THE SKY IS FULL OF SONG by Lee Bennett Hopkins, 1983. Used by permission of the author who controls all rights.

Hinshaw Music Inc. for *Here's to America* by Natalie Sleeth. Copyright © 1977 by Hinshaw Music, Inc.

Tony Hughes for *Little Blue Top* from POLLUTION OR ECOLOGY, published by Lutheran Church Press. Copyright © 1970 by Tony Hughes. Reprinted by permission.

Alfred A. Knopf, Inc. for *Dream Variations* by Langston Hughes. Copyright © 1926 by Alfred A. Knopf, Inc. and renewed 1954 by Langston Hughes. Reprinted from SELECTED POEMS OF LANGSTON HUGHES, by permission of Alfred A. Knopf, Inc.

MMB Music, Inc. for *Hey Concentration* from LET'S SLICE THE ICE by Eleanor Fulton and Pat Smith. Copyright © 1978 MMB Music, Inc., St. Louis. Used by permission. Unauthorized reproduction prohibited.

McGraw-Hill Ryerson Ltd. for *Hey Dum Diddeley Dum* by Marc Stone from ELEPHANT JAM. Copyright © 1980 Pachyderm Music. Reprinted by permission of McGraw-Hill Ryerson Ltd., Toronto.

Copyright © 1988 Macmillan Publishing Company, a division of Macmillan, Inc.

All rights reserved. No part of this book may be reproduced or transmitted in any form or by any means, electronic or mechanical, including photocopying, recording, or by any information storage and retrieval system, without permission in writing from the Publisher.

Macmillan Publishing Company
866 Third Avenue
New York, N.Y. 10022
Collier Macmillan Canada, Inc.

Printed in the United States of America

ISBN: 0-02-293370-0
9 8 7 6 5 4

Merkaz Letarbut Vechinuch for *Artsa Alinu*, a Jewish folk song from A TREASURY OF JEWISH FOLKSONGS, edited by Ruth Rubin. Reprinted courtesy of Merkaz Letarbut Vechinuch, Tel Aviv, Israel.

W. W. Norton & Company for *Song of the Fishes* from SONGS OF AMERICAN SAILORMEN, compiled by Joanna Colcord. Used by permission of W. W. Norton & Company, Inc. Copyright © 1938 by W. W. Norton & Company, Inc. Copyright renewed 1966 by The Boone County State Bank, Lebanon, Indiana, Executor of the Estate of the Author.

Noteman Press for "Low 'D' Boogie" and "High 'D' Boogie" from THE HARMONIOUS RECORDER (Soprano Book, Alto Book, Teacher's Edition) by Dorothy Gail Elliott. Used by permission of copyright owner, Noteman Press, 2603 Andrea Lane, Dallas, TX 75228.

Oxford University Press for *Cornish Wassail*, from SOCIABLE CAROLS by Anne Mendoza and Pat Shaw. © Oxford University Press, London, England, 1979. Reprinted by permission; and *Rattlesnake* from ENGLISH FOLKSONGS FROM THE SOUTHERN APPALACHIANS by Cecil Sharp, 1966. Reprinted by permission of Oxford University Press, London, England.

Prentice-Hall Inc. for *Hike Along* by Florence Martin from GROWING WITH MUSIC Series, Book 3 by Wilson, et al., Copyright © 1970, Prentice-Hall, Inc., Englewood Cliffs, NJ.

Reconstructionist Rabbinical College for *O Hanukah* (also titled *Hanukah Song*). Reprinted by permission of Judith Eisenstein.

Marian Reiner for *Winter Dark* from I THOUGHT I HEARD THE CITY by Lilian Moore. Copyright © 1969 by Lilian Moore. Reprinted and recorded by permission of Marian Reiner for the author.

Carroll A. Rinehart for *The First Noel*, 1978, and *I'm Gonna Sing*, 1979. Reprinted by permission of arranger, Carroll A. Rinehart.

Rockhaven Music for *Don Gato, Join Hands in Brotherhood, Ahrirang, Pass the Broomstick*. Copyright © 1986 and 1987.

Konnie Saliba for *My Good Old Man*. Used by permission of Konnie Saliba, Cock-A-Doodle Tunes Publisher, P.O. Box 311, Cordova, TN 38018.

Silver Burdett for *Zumba, Zumba* arranged by Francis Girard, words by Margaret Marks. Copyright © 1981 by Silver Burdett Company. All rights reserved. Used by permission.

Ben Snowball for *Eskimo Ice Cream* collected by Rita Blumenstein and Ben Snowball. Reprinted by permission of Benedict A. Snowball.

Stormking Music for *The Goat*, adapted by Alan Mills. Copyright © 1963 by Stormking Music Inc. All rights reserved. Used by permission.

Tiparm Music Co. for *Rattlin' Bog*, adapted by Joan, Tom, Pat, Liam Clancy and Tommy Makem, 1963. Reprinted by permission of Tiparm Music Co.

United Synagogue of America Commission on Jewish Education for *Who Can Retell?* translated by B. M. Edidin, music by M. Ravino, arranged by Harry Coopersmith. From THE SONGS WE SING edited by Harry Coopersmith. Reprinted by permission and published by the United Synagogue of America Commission on Jewish Education.

Jos Wuytack for *Funga Alafia*. Arranged by Jos Wuytack. Reprinted by permission of the arranger.

Some line drawings of musical instruments reprinted by permission of Harvard University Press from NEW HARVARD DICTIONARY OF MUSIC by Don M. Randel. Copyright 1987 by the President and Fellows of Harvard College.

LISTENING MAPS

The authors and publisher thank the following for creating these Listening Maps: Jacque Fowler, page 48; Dr. Thomas Ashbaugh, pages 167, 178-179.

PHOTO CREDITS:

AFTER IMAGE: © Dale R. Thompson, 86. CLARA AICH: 3, 4, 5, 12, 15, 19, 24TL,TR, 38, 51, 55, 57, 74, 79, 88, 103, 109, 123T, 159, 160, 172, 173LC, 178BR, 201T, 212, 266, 267. ANIMALS, ANIMALS: © Marcia W. Griffen, 43TR; © Richard Kolar, 43BR; © Joe McDonald, 43TL; © Ray Richardson, 43TC. ART RESOURCE/SCALA: Giraudon, 13TL; 168BR, 164–5. AVERY FISHER HALL: © Henry Grossinsky, 178TL, TR, 179BR. © VICTORIA BELLER-SMITH: 24B, 54, 64, 74B, 75TL, 114, 128, 158. © BETH BERGMAN: 127TR. THE BETTMAN ARCHIVE, INC.: 13R, 37, 68T, 89, 107, 132, 133T, B, 179TR, 209. BISHOP MUSEUM: 173T. LEE BOLTIN PICTURE LIBRARY: © Lee Boltin, 116L,R, 118. BRUCE COLEMAN, INC.: © Bob Gossington, 43BL; © Keith Gunnar, 43BC, 49; © Frank Obezle, 16. CULVER PICTURES: 145B. LEO DE WYS, INC.: © Messerschmidt, 144; © J. Schmied, 43C. MARJORY DRESSLER: 6T,B, 82, 83, 180–1, 204, 205. © FRANK DRIGGS: 145T. DRK PHOTOS: © Tom Bean, x–1B; 46–7B; © R.J. Erwin, 46T; © John Gerlach, 29TC; © Kelly Huffey, 1TR; © Johnny Johnson, 46–7TC, 98–9B; © Stephen J. Kraseman, x–1TC, 29TR, 156–7TC; © George J. Sanker, xT; © Tom Schneider, 99T; © Stephen Trimble, 58–9B. © FLAG RESEARCH CENTER: 134L,R, 135L. FOLIO, INC.: 69TL. F.P.G.: © M. Greenberg, 70. FREE LIBRARY OF PHILADELPHIA: 72. © GLOBUS BROTHERS: 142TC,C. © G.D. HACKETT: 201. COURTESY GEORGE HARRAP AND CO., LTD., London: From *African Music: A People's Art*, by Francis Bebey (1975), 173TR. THE IMAGE BANK: © Sonja Bullaty, 156–7B; © C. Chassagne, 169; © François Dardelet, 28TC; © Nicholas Foster, 28–9B, 157R; © Gary Gray, 68–9; © Anne Van Der Vaeren, 160–1; © Hans Wendler, 47T. JEREBOAM, INC.: © Jorge Ianiszewski, 173BR; © Brent Jones, 130L,R; © Lou Jones, 178BL. L.G.I.: © David Hathcox, 137. MAGNUM PHOTOS, INC.: © Erich Hartmann, 130C; © Alex Webb, 203. THE METROPOLITAN MUSEUM OF ART: The Crosby Brown Collection of Musical Instruments (1889), 172. © LAWRENCE MIGDALE: 179BL, 187R. COURTESY MUSEUM OF FINE ARTS, Boston: Rebuilt by François Etienne Blanchet, Paris, 1758; Rebuilt by Rascal Taskin, Paris, 1781; Painted poplar, spruce, and other woods; Length: 2218 mm. Width: 929 mm.
(Photo credits continued on page 277)

v

AUTHORS

Barbara Staton has taught music at all levels, kindergarten through college, and for eight years was music television teacher for the State of Georgia. She is author of a four-volume series of books and records designed to teach music concepts through movement. She holds a B.S. degree in Music Education and an M.A. in Dance and Related Arts. Mrs. Staton has written numerous songs for television and recordings and is a composer member of ASCAP.

Dr. Merrill Staton earned his M.A. and Ed.D. degrees from Teachers College, Columbia University, and is nationally known as a music educator, choral conductor, singer, composer, and record producer. He has been music director and has conducted the Merrill Staton Voices on many network TV series and recordings. Dr. Staton has been a leader in the field of music education for the past twenty-five years, and pioneered the use of children's voices on recordings for education.

Marilyn Davidson teaches elementary general music in Pequannock, New Jersey. She also teaches graduate summer courses in music education at Potsdam University of New York; the Hartt School of Music at the University of Hartford in West Hartford, Connecticut; and Teachers College, Columbia University, in New York City. Her teaching experience spans twenty-eight years at all levels.

Dr. Phyllis Kaplan received her Ph.D. in Music Education from the University of Michigan. She has taught in the Ohio public schools and at Kent State and Penn State universities. She has served on the MENC National Committee on Music Education for Handicapped Learners. Currently, she is Coordinator of Elementary General Music for the Montgomery County Public Schools, Rockville, Maryland. She is on the Music Educators Journal Editorial Board.

Dr. Susan Snyder has taught general music for fifteen years. She holds a Ph.D. in Curriculum and Instruction and an Orff Master Teacher's Certificate. She has worked with preschool and handicapped children and has done extensive study in aesthetics, early childhood, and the Kodály method. Currently, Dr. Snyder is teaching in the Greenwich, Connecticut, public schools. She is an adjunct professor at Teachers College, Columbia University, directing the Ridgewood Summer Program.

SPECIAL CONTRIBUTORS

Dr. Betty Atterbury
Mainstreaming

Marshia Beck
Movement

Mary Frances Early
Black American Music

Joan Gregoryk
Vocal Development

János Horváth
Kodály

Virginia Mead
Dalcroze

Mollie Tower
Listening Selections

CONSULTANTS AND CONTRIBUTING WRITERS

Dr. Betty Atterbury, University of Southern Maine, Gorham, Maine ● **Marshia Beck,** Holy Names College, Oakland, California ● **Diane Bennette,** Bergenfield Public Schools, Bergenfield, New Jersey ● **Teri Burdette,** Barnsley Elementary, Rockville, Maryland ● **Dr. Robert A. Duke,** University of Texas, Austin, Texas ● **Mary Frances Early,** Atlanta Public Schools, Atlanta, Georgia ● **Nancy Ferguson,** University of Arizona, Tucson, Arizona ● **Diane Fogler,** Rockaway Township Public Schools, Rockaway, New Jersey ● **Joan Gregoryk,** Chevy Chase Elementary, Chevy Chase, Maryland ● **János Horváth,** University of Calgary, Calgary, Alberta, Canada ● **Dr. Judith A. Jellison,** University of Texas, Austin, Texas ● **Dr. JaFran Jones,** Bowling Green State University, Bowling Green, Ohio ● **James Kenward,** Howe Avenue Elementary, Sacramento, California ● **Tom Kosmala,** Pittsburgh Public Schools, Pittsburgh, Pennsylvania ● **Virginia Mead,** Kent State University, Kent, Ohio ● **Belle San Miguel-Ortiz,** San Antonio Independent School District, San Antonio, Texas ● **Jane Pippart,** Lancaster Public Schools, Lancaster, Pennsylvania ● **Dr. Susan Snyder,** Hamilton Avenue Elementary, Greenwich, Connecticut ● **Mollie Tower,** Austin Independent School District, Austin, Texas

contents

UNIT 1

OUR MUSICAL WORLD

Farther Than Far

I look into the sky and see
The leafy branches of a tree,
And higher still a bird in flight,
And higher still a cloud of white.
Beyond the cloud is lots more sky,
Farther than far, higher than high.
And where it ends, another place
Is filled with space and space and space.

—*Margaret Hillert*

1

PAT, WALK, AND PLAY THE BEAT

The beat in this song looks like this:

These notes are **quarter notes.** Each sounds for one beat.

- Listen to the song and pat the beat.
- Walk the beat and play it on classroom instruments.

Hey Dum Diddeley Dum

Words and music by Marc Stone

3. Ev'ryone come and sing,
   With a hey dum diddeley dum.
   We're gonna make these old rafters ring with our
   Hey dum diddeley dum.
   Refrain

You can play long sounds on most instruments. Figure out how to play a sound that lasts two beats.

A sound that lasts two beats looks like this $\text{\musHalf}$ in the pattern below. It is called a **half note**.

- Clap this pattern as you sing the refrain of "Hey Dum Diddeley Dum."

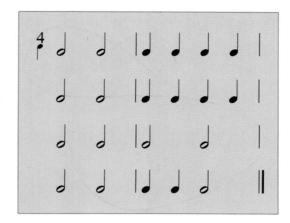

- Play the above pattern on instruments with "Hey Dum Diddeley Dum." Play half notes on the tambourine. Play quarter notes on a wood instrument.

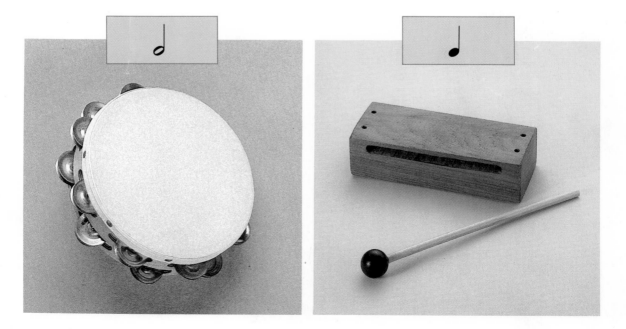

THE WOODWIND FAMILY

The **woodwinds** are one of four instrument families in the orchestra. Members of this family include the flute, piccolo, clarinet, saxophone, oboe, English horn, and bassoon. These instruments are called woodwinds because they were originally made of wood. You play them by blowing air (wind) through them. Today, some woodwinds are still made of wood. Others are made of plastic or metal.

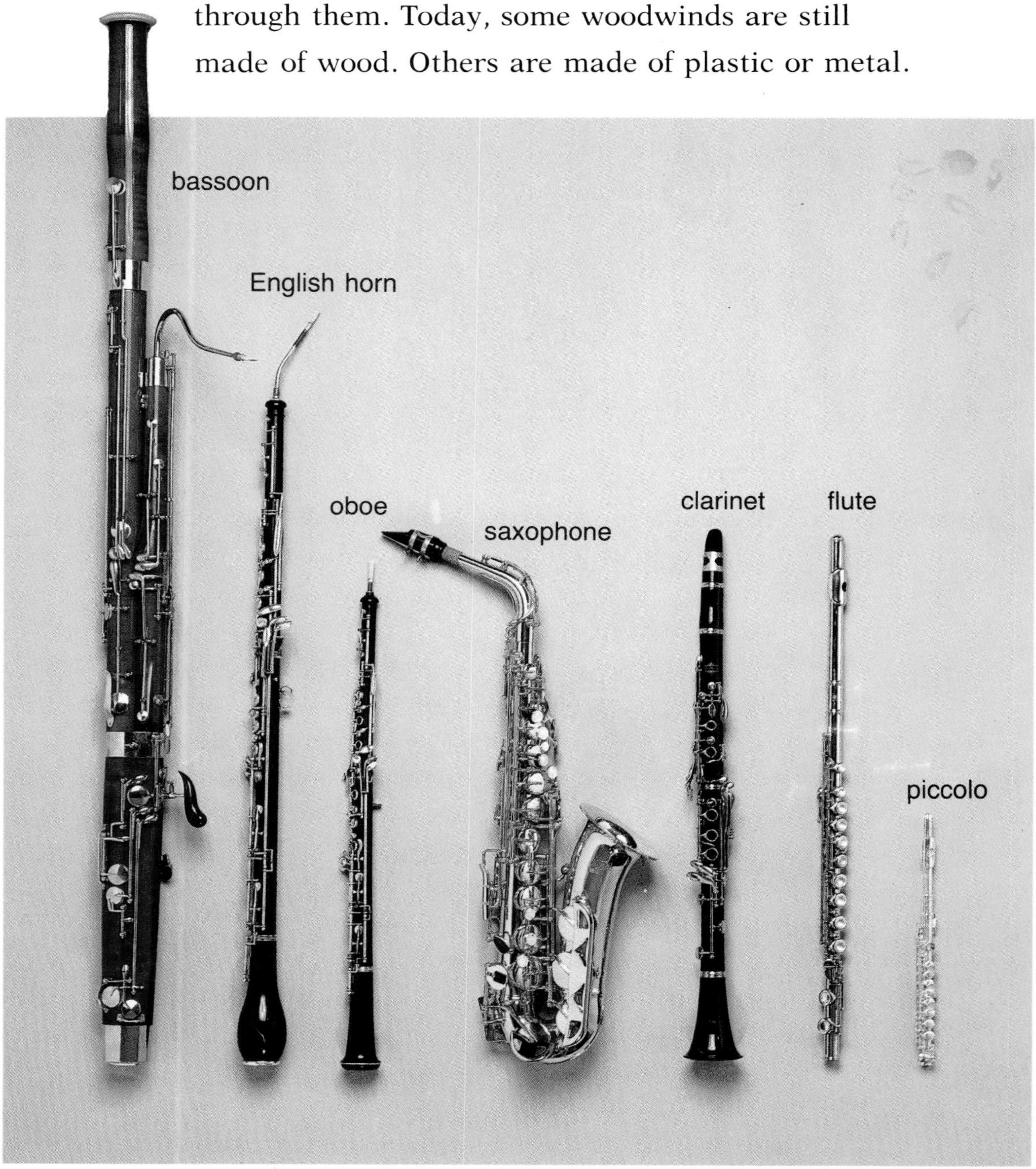

bassoon

English horn

oboe

saxophone

clarinet

flute

piccolo

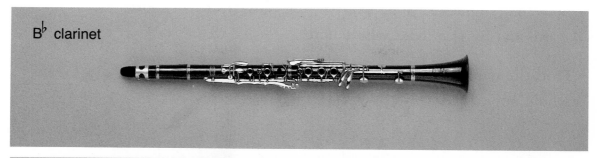

B♭ clarinet

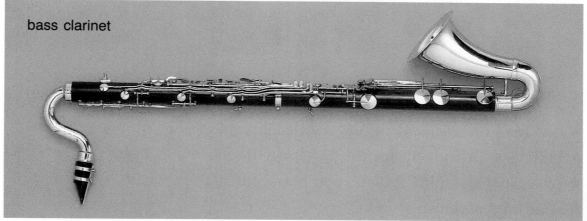

bass clarinet

There are different kinds of clarinets. Two are shown above.
The B♭ clarinet is the most common.

Clarinets use a reed to produce a sound.

reed

reed on mouthpiece

How do you think a reed helps make the sound?

- Count to 4, but pat only on 1.

A note that sounds for four beats in the pattern below looks like this **o** . It is called a **whole note.**

- Find the quarter notes. Find the half notes. Find the whole note.

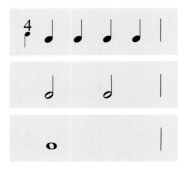

- Choose an instrument to represent each kind of note.
- Play your instrument for the pattern with your notes in it.
- Listen to "Oomph Fah Fah" and play your pattern when your note is shown.

"Oomph Fah Fah," by Ellis Larkins, played by Benny Goodman

● Pat the beat as you sing this song.

The Boatmen's Dance

American Minstrel Song

1. The boat-men dance, The boat-men sing, The boat-men up to ev-'ry-thing.

And when the boat-man gets on shore, He spends his cash and works for more.

Refrain

Then dance, the boat-men, dance! Oh, dance, the boat-men, dance! Oh,

dance all night till the broad day-light, And go home with your pals in the morn-ing.

2. The oyster boat should keep to the shore,
   The fishing smack should venture more,
   The schooner sails before the wind,
   The steamboat leaves a streak behind.
   Refrain

3. When you go to the boatmen's ball,
   Dance with your wife or not at all,
   Skyblue jacket and tarpaulin hat,
   Look out, my boys, for the nine-tail cat.
   Refrain

FIND THE PHRASES

A **phrase** is a complete musical thought. Phrases
are marked in music with an arc.

- Move your arm in an arc to show each phrase in "He's Got
  the Whole World in His Hands."
- Sing each phrase as a musical thought.

He's Got the Whole World in His Hands

Black American Spiritual

2. He's got the wind and rain in His hands,
   He's got the wind and rain in His hands,
   He's got the wind and rain in His hands,
   He's got the whole world in His hands.

● Move your arm in an arc to show each phrase.

Deep and Wide

Traditional

Deep and wide, deep and wide,

There's a foun-tain flow-ing deep and wide, _____

Deep and wide, deep and wide,

There's a foun-tain flow-ing deep and wide.

● Listen for the high and low sounds of the B♭ clarinet.

 "Piece IV," from *Four Pieces for Clarinet and Piano,* by Alban Berg (äl′bän berk)

ALBAN BERG

Alban Berg was born in 1885 in Austria. His music is different sounding. The melodies have wide skips. The steady beat is hard to feel. His best-known composition is the opera *Wozzeck.*

UPWARD AND DOWNWARD MELODIES

● Find where the melody in this song moves upward,
  downward, and stays the same.

The Rattlin' Bog

Irish Folk Song

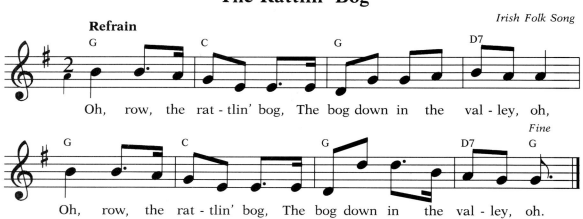

Refrain

Oh,   row,   the rat - tlin' bog,   The bog down in   the   val - ley, oh,

Fine

Oh,   row,   the rat - tlin' bog,   The bog down in   the val - ley, oh.

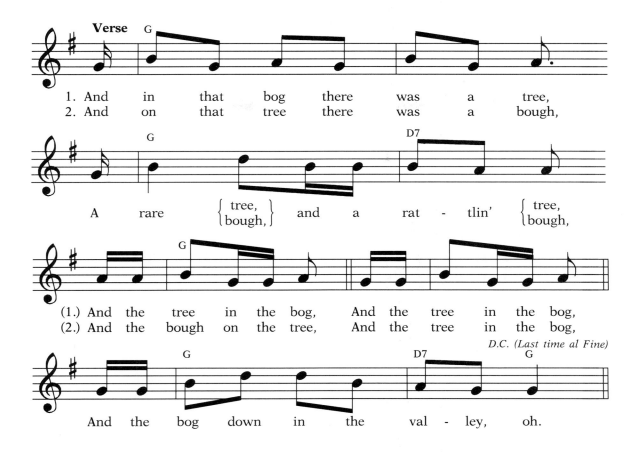

Verse G

1. And in that bog there was a tree,
2. And on that tree there was a bough,

A rare { tree, bough, } and a rat-tlin' { tree, bough,

(1.) And the tree in the bog, And the tree in the bog,
(2.) And the bough on the tree, And the tree in the bog,

D.C. (Last time al Fine)

And the bog down in the val-ley, oh.

3. Now on that bough there was a branch,
A rare branch, and a rattlin' branch,
And the branch on the bough,
And the bough on the tree,
And the tree in the bog,
And the bog down in the valley, oh.
Refrain

4. Now on the branch there was a nest,
A rare nest, and a rattlin' nest,
And the nest on the branch,
And the branch on the bough,
And the bough on the tree,
And the tree in the bog,
And the bog down in the valley, oh.
Refrain

5. Now in the nest there was a bird,
A rare bird, and a rattlin' bird,
And the bird in the nest,
And the nest on the branch . . .
Refrain

6. And on that bird there was a tail . . .
Refrain

11

Sometimes instruments or singers take turns playing or singing. They have a **musical conversation.**

- Listen to a conversation between a clarinet and stringed instruments.
- Move your hands to show the direction of the melody line. Move your left hand when you hear the strings. Move your right hand when you hear the clarinet.

Clarinet Quintet in A Major
by Wolfgang Amadeus Mozart

The Mozart Family, by Carmontelle, shows young Mozart with his father and sister.

WOLFGANG AMADEUS MOZART

Wolfgang Amadeus Mozart (vôlf′gäng ä-mä-dā′əs mōt′särt) was born in Salzburg, Austria, in 1756. When Mozart was three, his father recognized that Mozart had unusual musical ability. Young Mozart learned to play the harpsichord at age 4 and then the violin. By the time he was 5, Mozart was composing his own music. Mozart's talent was so extraordinary that he was asked to play his music throughout the capitals of Europe. By the time he was 20, Mozart had traveled all over Europe and was quite well known.

After settling in Vienna, Mozart continued to compose. His music includes many different styles. Although he only lived to be 35, Mozart produced more than 25 string quartets, 20 operas, 40 symphonies, and 17 piano sonatas.

13

INTRODUCING G, A, AND B

● Listen for the two sections in the song.

Oh, Won't You Sit Down?

Black American Spiritual

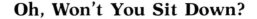

Oh, won't you sit down? _ Lord, I can't sit down. _

Oh, won't you sit down? _ Lord, I can't sit down. _

Oh, won't you sit down? _ Lord, I can't sit down. _

'Cause I just got to Heav-en, gon-na look a-round. _

1. Who's that yon-der dressed in red? _ Must be the chil-dren that _ Mo-ses led. _

D.C. (Last time al Fine)

Who's that yon-der dressed in white? _ Must be the chil-dren of the Is-rael-ite. _

2. Who's that yonder dressed in blue?
   Must be the children that are comin' through.
   Who's that yonder dressed in black?
   Must be the hypocrites a-turn-in' back. *Refrain*

14

The **staff** is made up of five lines and four spaces. Notes are written on the staff and their pitches are named by the first seven letters of the alphabet. Notice where the pitches G, A, and B are located on the staff.

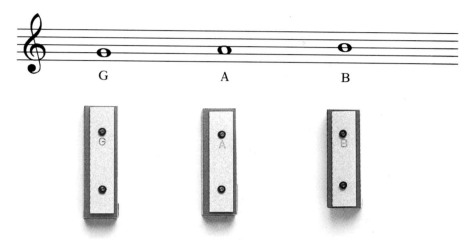

- Play G, A, and B on bells. Try to make a song.
- Find G, A, and B in "Oh, Won't You Sit Down?"
- Play B and G over and over to make a cuckoo's sound.
- Listen for this cuckoo sound in "The Cuckoo."

"The Cuckoo," from *The Carnival of the Animals,* by Camille Saint-Saëns (kä-mē´yə saN-säN´)

TWO SOUNDS ON ONE BEAT

Some names have only one syllable.

● Think of someone in your class with a one-syllable name.
  Say the name four times as you clap quarter notes.

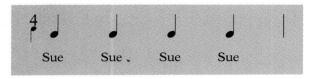

Some names have two syllables.

● Think of someone in your class with a two-syllable name.
  If you clap quarter notes, you will say one of the syllables
  without clapping.

● Clap and say the two-syllable name
  four times. Clap every syllable.
  Now you are clapping
  eighth notes. They look
  like this ♫ .

- Find the eighth notes in this song.

Turn the Glasses Over

American Singing Game

I've been to Haar - lem, I've been to Do - ver,

I've trav - eled this wide world all o - ver,

O - ver, o - ver, three times o - ver,

Drink what you have to drink and turn the glass - es o - ver.

Sail - ing east, sail - ing west,

Sail - ing o - ver the o - cean,

Bet - ter watch out when the boat be - gins to rock,

Or you'll lose your girl in the o - cean.

USING G, A, AND B

This song is a musical conversation.

● What is the first question? What is the first answer?

Who Built the Ark?

Black American Spiritual

Solo G — Who built the ark? Group D7 — No - ah, No - ah,

Solo G — Who built the ark? Group — Bro - ther G D7 No - ah G built the ark. *Fine*

Group G
1. Now didn't old No - ah build the ark?____
2. He built it long, both wide and tall,____

G — Built it out of a hick-o-ry bark.__
Plen-ty of room for the

[1. D7 G]
[2. D7 G *D.C. al Fine*] large__ and small.__

● Play B on the recorder.

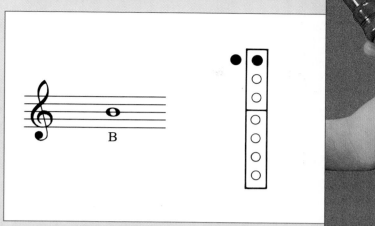

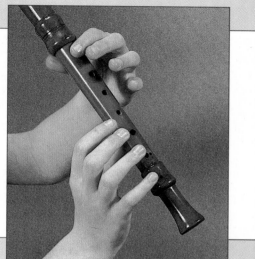

● Play A.

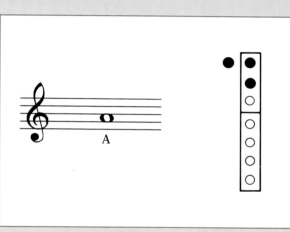

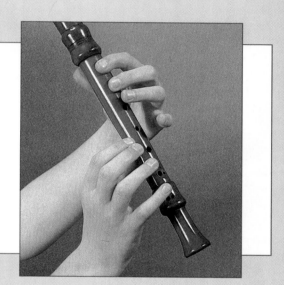

● Play G.

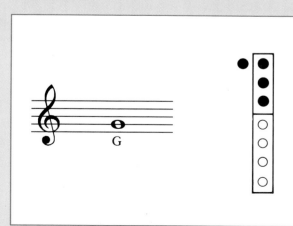

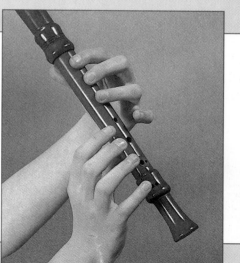

LONG AND SHORT SOUNDS

Jump rope is a game that can be played in many different ways. You can jump rope all by yourself while you say a rhyme to the beat, or two people can turn the rope and say a rhyme while a third person jumps. You and your friends may have your own way of jumping rope.

Have you ever played Double Dutch? Double Dutch is a difficult and fast way of jumping rope. In this game, two ropes are turned at the same time but not together. Because it is so fast, there is very little time to think as one rope follows the other.

When you see $\overset{\times}{|}$ in the music, you speak the words instead of singing them.

● Tap the beat with your feet.

Hey Concentration

Double Dutch Jump Rope

C

Hey con - cen - tra - tion   where have you been   a - round the   cor - ner and

G7   C

back   a - gain   stole   my   mon - ey   stole   my   hon - ey   Ma -

G7   C   *spoken*

- ma's got the hic - cups   Dad - dy's got the flu. Now   come on   boys __ Let's

slice the ice   slice it   1   slice it 2   slice it   3   4   5 __ slice it   6   slice it 7   slice it

G   C   G

8 9 10 __   Hey   ev - 'ry - bod - y   come on and do your thing.   2 up

bop, bop   2 down   bop, bop   2 up   bop, bop   2 down   bop, bop   2 up.

21

FORM

● Find the two sections in this song.

Little Blue Top

Refrain

Words and music by Tony Hughes

Round and round goes the lit - tle blue top,

Whirl - ing and turn - ing with nev - er a stop;

Dap - pled with white, dap - pled with brown, ___

The lit - tle blue top keeps a - turn - ing a - round. ___

Verse

1. O, there's wild rag - ing o - ceans and proud moun - tain chains,

Green peace-ful val-leys and wide grass-y plains,

Fam'-lies of life ___ that each set-ting con - tains,

Dol - phins and spi - ders and ti - gers and cranes.

2. O, there's teachers and lawyers and medicine men,
Places to go to and people who've been;
Others who stay home and tend to the shop,
And they all whirl and turn on the little blue top. *Refrain*

3. But there're men who are greedy and men who don't care,
And they're fouling our rivers and poisoning our air.
If all of the rest of us don't make 'em stop,
They might end all the life on the little blue top. *Refrain*

HAVE A MUSICAL CONVERSATION

"Who Built the Ark?" is a musical conversation. There is
a question and an answer.

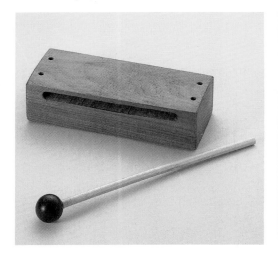

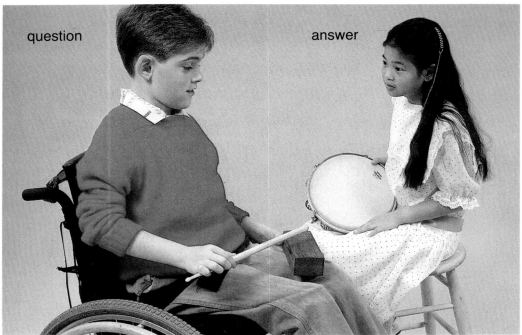

question   answer

- Have a musical conversation with another person. Choose
  an instrument. One person plays a question. The other
  person plays an answer.
- Listen to your partner's question. Use part of it in your
  answer.

The Gossips, Norman Rockwell. © 1948 courtesy of The Estate of Norman Rockwell

This painting by Norman Rockwell is called *The Gossips*. Norman Rockwell was a popular American artist and illustrator. His paintings were usually of everyday people and often told a humorous story. Many of his paintings were used as cover illustrations for magazines, especially *The Saturday Evening Post*.

Rockwell was born in New York City in 1894 and was a professional artist by the time he was sixteen. He died in 1978.

TAKE ANOTHER LOOK

Our Musical World

Turn the Glasses Over

Oh, Won't You Sit Down?

Hey Concentration

The Boatmen's Dance

● Oomph Fah Fah

● The Cuckoo

Little Blue Top

Hey Dum Diddeley Dum

Do you remember?

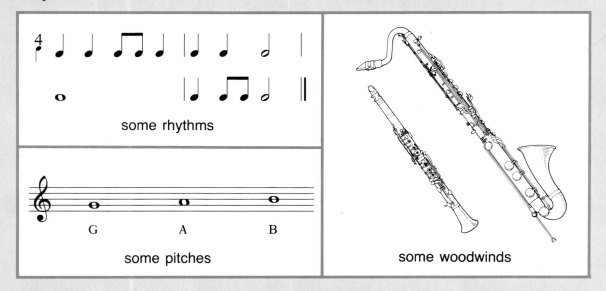

some rhythms

some pitches

some woodwinds

JUST CHECKING

1. Find the instrument that belongs to the woodwind family.

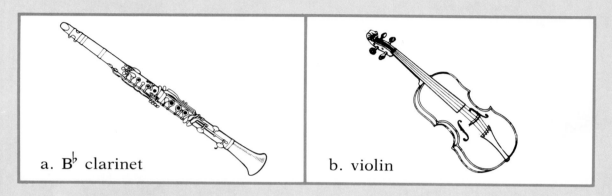

a. B♭ clarinet

b. violin

2. Find the quarter note.

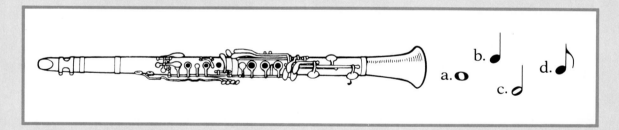

a. 𝅝   b. ♩   c. ♩   d. ♪

3. Find the longest sounding note.

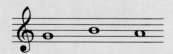

a.   b.   c. 𝅝

4. Give the letter name of each pitch.

UNIT 2 CHANGES

PITCH

- Use your finger to trace the upward and downward path of the notes on the staff.

Hike Along

Hungarian Folk Song
Words by Florence Martin

1. Take a pack and we'll go hik - ing,
   There's a stream that's ev - er wind - ing

Find a hid - den path - way in the woods we know.
To a gold - en mead - ow as the soft winds blow.

Sing - ing, sing - ing as we go a - long;

Foot - steps ech - o - ing our hik - ing song.

2. Climb to where the clouds are passing
   Close enough to touch a field of new-mown hay.
   Singing, singing as we go along,
   Footsteps echoing our hiking song.
   Down below a bright spring ripples,
   Soon the valley beckons and we're on our way.

- Move your body to show the direction of the melody as you sing.

Miss Mary Mack

Black American Play-party Song

1. Miss Ma - ry Mack, Mack, Mack,

All dressed in black, black, black,

With sil - ver but - tons, but - tons, but - tons,

All down her back, back, back.

2. She asked her mother, mother, mother,
For fifty cents, cents, cents,
To see the cows, cows, cows,
Jump over the fence, fence, fence.

3. They jumped so high, high, high,
They reached the sky, sky, sky,
And never came back, back, back,
Till the fourth of July, lie, lie!

What is the letter name of the highest pitch on this staff?

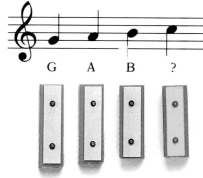

G A B ?

- Play the notes on the bells.
- Find these pitches in the song.
- Compare these bells with the piano keyboard inside the back cover of the book. Which two bells will have no black key between them? They are a **half step** apart. The other pitches are a **whole step** apart.

THE METER SIGNATURE

When the beats of a song are grouped in sets of two, the song is in $\frac{2}{4}$ meter. The **meter signature** at the beginning of each song shows how the beats are grouped in measures.

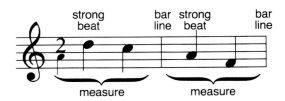

The number at the top tells how many beats are in each measure.

The note on the bottom tells what kind of note is equal to one beat.

When a 2 is at the top, you can expect a strong beat on every other beat.

● Tap the beats in this meter. Make the first beat of each measure the strong beat.

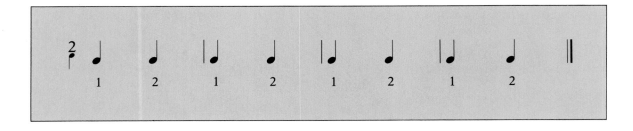

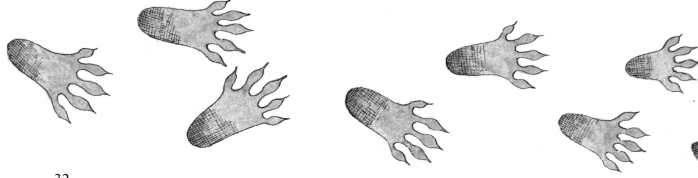

ROUND THE ROCK

Round and round the rugged rock
the ragged rascal ran.

- Say the tongue-twister words one sound to each beat.

  Tap the beat.

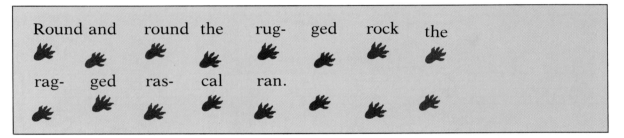

| Round | and | round | the | rug- | ged | rock | the |
| rag- | ged | ras- | cal | ran. | | | |

- Say it again. Stretch each sound to last two beats.

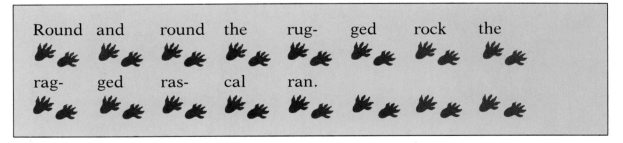

| Round | and | round | the | rug- | ged | rock | the |
| rag- | ged | ras- | cal | ran. | | | |

- Say it again. Shrink it by saying two sounds for every beat.

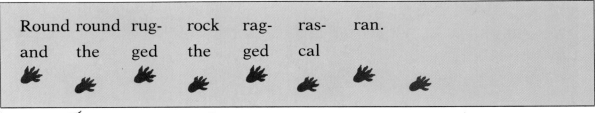

| Round | round | rug- | rock | rag- | ras- | ran. |
| and | the | ged | the | ged | cal | |

33

- Sing this song about Old Abram Brown.

Old Abram Brown

Music by Benjamin Britten

Old A - bram Brown is dead and gone,

We'll nev - er see him more.

He used to wear an old gray coat

All but - toned down be - fore.

New Looks for Old Abram Brown

- Sing "Old Abram Brown" making each note twice as long.
- Sing "Old Abram Brown" making each note half as long.

OLD ABRAM BROWN
34   Text by Walter de la Mare from *Tom Tiddler's Ground.* Music by Benjamin Britten. © Copyright 1936 by Boosey & Co. Ltd.; Renewed 1963. Reprinted by permission of Boosey & Hawkes, Inc.

- Pretend to shear the sheep as you sing. Make one
  movement for every strong beat.

Sheep Shearing

Swedish Folk Song

1. Go get the sheep, we're clip - ping to - day,
2. Tell Moth - er dear we're card - ing to - day,

Clip - ping their wool, yes, clip - ping their wool
Card - ing the wool, yes, card - ing the wool

So we can knit some stock - ings for you,
So we can knit a scarf for her, too,

Then we shall dance till morn - ing.
Then we shall dance till morn - ing.

Refrain

Surr, surr, surr, surr, surr, surr, Wheel spins a-round, now hear the sound;

Surr, surr, surr, surr, surr, surr, Then we shall dance till morn-ing.

- What does the number at the beginning of the song tell
  you about how the beats are grouped?

CHANGES IN RHYTHM

What is the meter signature of this camp song?

● Find these rhythm patterns in the song.

Rally Song

Balkan Round

Mil - ha   bi   lou   lou - bi   shem - bel,

Mil - ha   bi   lou   lou - bi   shem - bel,

Mil - ha   bi   lou   lou - bi   shem - bel,

Mil - ha   bi   lou   lou - bi   shem - bel.

- Listen and pat the strong beat on your lap. Clap all the other beats.

The pattern looks like this:

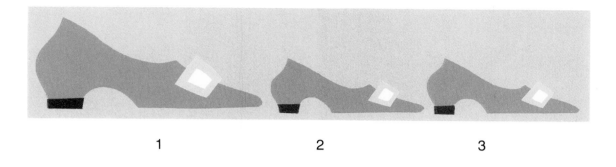

1   2   3

 "Minuetto," from *L'Arlésienne,* by Georges Bizet (zhôrzh bē-zā')

A **minuet** (min-yə-wet') is a stately French court dance. It is in $\frac{3}{}$ meter. **Minuetto** is the Italian word for minuet. The minuet was first danced about 300 years ago.

Dancing the Minuet

SAXOPHONES

soprano
saxophone

alto
saxophone

tenor
saxophone

baritone
saxophone

38

The **saxophone** is a member of the woodwind family, but it is not made of wood. It is made of metal. The sound of the saxophone is made by blowing across a single reed attached to the mouthpiece. There are four different saxophones. From smallest to largest they are the soprano, alto, tenor, and baritone. The smaller saxophones play higher pitches than the larger saxophones.

- Look at the pictures. Decide which saxophone can play the highest pitches and which can play the lowest pitches.
- Listen for the saxophone in "Minuetto," by Bizet.

- Pat the beat as you sing "Pass the Broomstick." Does this song move in sets of three like "Minuetto," or in sets of two?

Pass the Broomstick

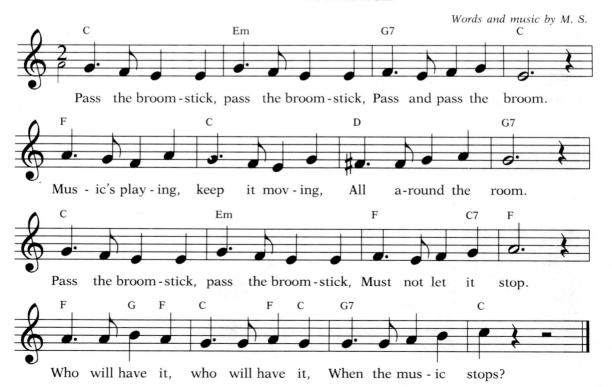

Words and music by M. S.

Pass the broom-stick, pass the broom-stick, Pass and pass the broom.

Mus-ic's play-ing, keep it mov-ing, All a-round the room.

Pass the broom-stick, pass the broom-stick, Must not let it stop.

Who will have it, who will have it, When the mus-ic stops?

39

GHOSTLY RHYTHMS

- Show how long a whole note lasts by doing this pattern.

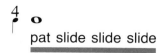

pat slide slide slide

- Show how long a half note lasts by doing this pattern.

pat slide pat slide

- Move to show how long each note lasts in this pattern.

- What is the meter signature of this song?

The Wobblin' Goblin

Music by Gerald Marks
Words by Milton Pascal

1. The wob - blin' gob - lin with the bro - ken broom _____ could nev - er fly too high, _____ For ev - 'ry time he'd take off, an - oth - er piece would break off, And soon he would be
2. Each eve - ning just as he would leave the ground, _____ his ra - di - o would say, _____ "Con - trol _ tow-er to gob - lin, your broom - stick is wob - blin', You'd bet - ter make a

dang-lin' in the sky. _____ It soon got so he could
land-ing right a - way." _____

on - ly ride when the witch - es took him pig-gy back; ____

Un - til one day he used his brain and bought him-self an aer-o - plane. _

3. So if you look for him on Hal-low-een, _ you'll see him zip and zoom, _

No harm can be-fall him; no long - er can they call him,

The wob - blin' gob - lin with the bro - ken broom. _____

COURTESY TRUSTEES OF THE NATIONAL GALLERY OF ART, London. *Ruins of a Castle*—Hobbema, 1629

Ruins of a Castle, by Meindert Hobbema

- Tell how the artist has used color to create the mood of this painting.

The musical piece called "The Old Castle" was inspired by a painting similar to the one above.

Each instrument has its own special sound, called **tone color.**

- Listen to two recordings of this music. Tell how a composer can use tone color to help create a mood.

 "The Old Castle," from *Pictures at an Exhibition,* by Modest Mussorgsky (mō-dest′ moo-sôrg′skē)

DYNAMIC CHANGES

- In the pictures below, what would sound the softest? the loudest?
- Tell how the sound of the hikers would change as they walked farther and farther away.

TAKE ANOTHER LOOK

Changes

Miss Mary Mack

Pass the Broomstick

Sheep Shearing

Old Abram Brown

Hike Along

● Minuetto

Do you remember?

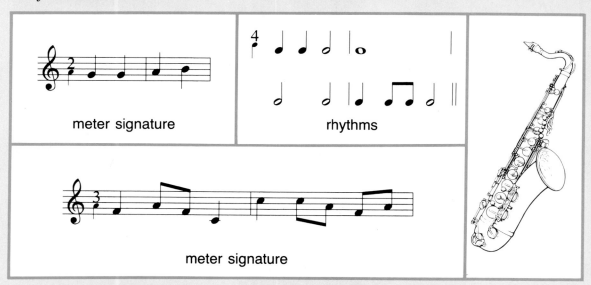

meter signature

rhythms

meter signature

JUST CHECKING

1. Which is a saxophone?

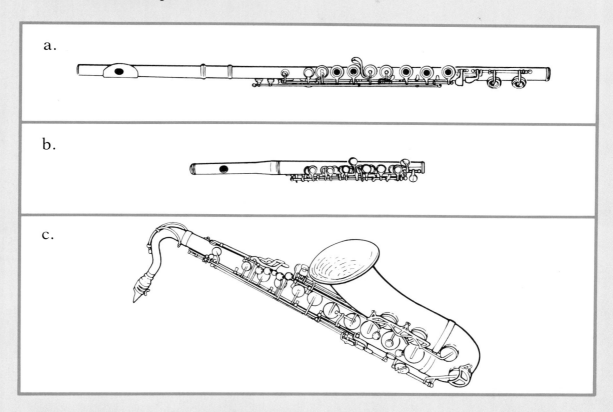

   a.

   b.

   c.

2. How many beats are in each measure?

3. How many beats are in each measure?

4. Does this music move in sets of two or sets of three?

UNIT 3 SOARING

I Go Forth to Move
About the Earth

I go forth to move about the earth,
I go forth as the owl, wise and knowing.
I go forth as the eagle, powerful and bold.
I go forth as the dove, peaceful and gentle.
I go forth to move about the earth
  in wisdom, courage, and peace.

—Alonzo Lopez

47

FORTISSIMO AND PIANISSIMO

The musical word for very loud is **fortissimo** (fôr-tis'ə-mō).
The symbol for this word is **ff.**

The musical word for very soft is **pianissimo** (pē-ə-nis'ə-mō).
The symbol for this word is **pp.**

- As you listen to "Cloudburst," find the symbols for
  fortissimo and *pianissimo* in the listening map below.

"Cloudburst," from *Grand Canyon Suite,* by Ferde Grofé
(fərd'ē grō-fā')

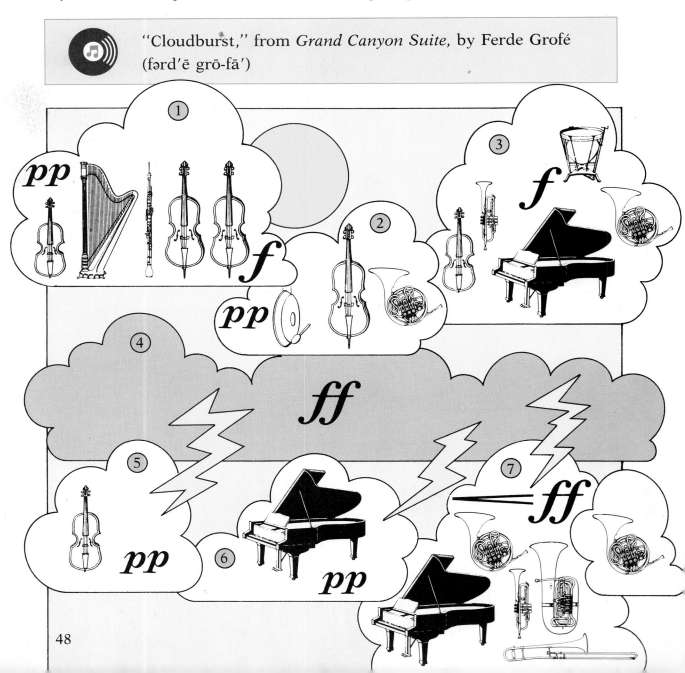

This song might be sung in a very quiet place. The sound of the paddle dipping into the water would seem loud in such a quiet place.

● Play a *pianissimo* drum beat with this song.

Canoe Song

Words and music by
Margaret Embers McGee

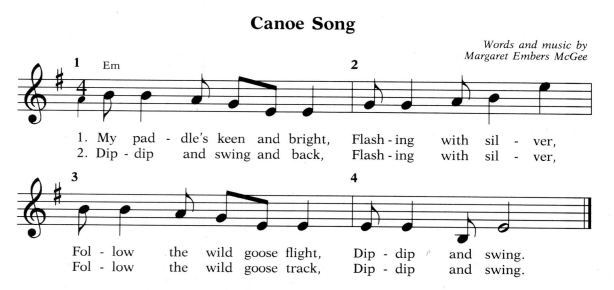

1. My pad - dle's keen and bright, Flash - ing with sil - ver,
2. Dip - dip and swing and back, Flash - ing with sil - ver,

Fol - low the wild goose flight, Dip - dip and swing.
Fol - low the wild goose track, Dip - dip and swing.

Dogies are motherless calves. On a trail drive, it is very quiet at night. The dogies can be scared even by the quietest sound. The cowboys sing to keep them calm.

● Sing this song as a night herder would.

Night Herding Song

American Cowboy Song

1. Oh, slow up, do-gies, quit rov-ing a-round, you have
2. I've cir-cle herd-ed and night herd-ed too, but to

wan-dered and tram-pled all o-ver the ground; Oh, graze a-long, do-gies, and
keep you to-geth-er, that's what I can't do; My horse is leg wea-ry, and

feed kind-a slow, and don't for-ev-er be on the go. Oh,
I'm aw-ful tired, but if you get a-way, I am sure to get fired. Bunch

move slow, do-gies, move slow, ___ Hi-oh, hi-oh-hi-oh! ___
up, lit-tle do-gies, bunch up, ___ Hi-oh, hi-oh-hi-oh! ___

WESTERN RHYTHMS

Saying words with rhythms can help you to remember the rhythms. "Western" words fit easily into $\frac{2}{4}$. meter.

- Each of these is a one-beat unit. Clap each unit four times.

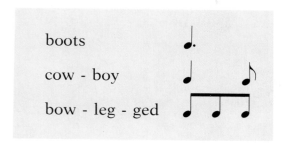

One-beat units can be combined to make longer rhythm patterns. Each pattern is four beats long.

- Say the words as you clap each pattern twice.

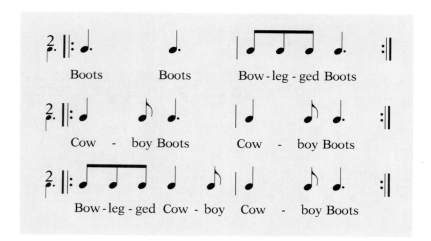

- Play these rhythm patterns on instruments such as these.

● Listen for the different rhythm patterns in this song.

Grandma's Feather Bed

Words and music by Jim Connor

1. Now when I was a lit-tle bit-ty boy Just up off _ of the floor, We used _ to go out to Grand-ma's house ev-'ry month end or so. _ _____ We'd have chick-en pie, _ and coun-try ham, and home-made but-ter on the bread. But the best darn thing a-bout

Grand-ma's house was a great big feath-er bed. It was nine feet high and

six feet wide and soft as a down-y chick. It was made from the feath-ers of

for-ty 'lev-en geese, took a whole bolt of cloth for the tick. It-'d

hold eight kids and four ____ hound dogs and the pig-gy we took from the

shed. We did-n't get much sleep, but we had a lot of fun on

Grand-ma's feath-er bed. (And) bed. (Well I) bed.

2. And after supper we'd sit around the fire
   And the old folks bit the shoe,
   And my Pa would talk about the farm
     and the war
   And my Granny'd sing a ballad or two.
   And I'd sit and listen and watch the fire,
   Till the cobwebs filled my head,
   The next thing I know I'll wake up in
     the mornin'
   In the middle of the old feather bed.

   Refrain

3. Well, I love my Ma, I love my Pa,
   I love a Granny and a Grandpa too,
   I been fishin' with my Uncle
   And I wrassle with my Cousin,
   I even kissed Aunt Lou (Phew!)
   But if I ever had to make a choice
   I guess it ought to be said
   That I'd trade them all
   Plus the gal down the road
   For Grandma's feather bed.

   Refrain

THE FLUTE AND PICCOLO

The flute and piccolo are members of the woodwind family. Flutes and piccolos were once made of wood but are now usually made of metal. There are silver flutes, gold flutes, and even crystal flutes.

The flute can play many pitches from high to low. The piccolo is half the size of a flute and plays an **octave,** or eight notes, higher. The higher notes are very piercing and can be heard above the entire orchestra. The tone colors of flutes and piccolos vary at different pitch levels.

To make a sound like a flute player does, you can blow across the top of an open bottle.

Big bottles produce low pitches and small bottles produce higher pitches. You can change the pitch by adding water to each bottle.

- Does adding water make the pitch higher or lower? Why?

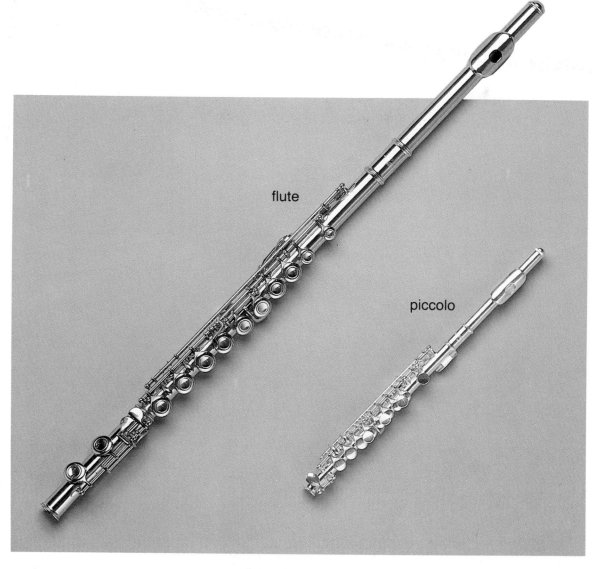

flute

piccolo

Different kinds of flutes are included among the folk instruments of many cultures around the world. The first flutes were played by blowing across a set of hollow reeds. These flutes were called panpipes. The recorder is related to the flute. You make a sound by blowing *into* the mouthpiece.

- Listen to many of the different sounds the flute and piccolo can make.

 Sounds of the flute and piccolo

- Raise your hand when you hear the flute.

Indian Lullaby

Quinault Indian Song

Oh lit-tle ba-by, ay-yo-yo, _ go to sleep now, ay-yo-yo. _

Fine

Slum-ber soft-ly, ay-yo-yo, _ slum-ber soft-ly, _ ay-yo-yo, _ a-yo-yo.

Oh lit-tle ba-by, bah-ah-ah-ah, ay-yo-yo, _ close your eyes, _ ay-yo-yo.

D.C. al Fine

Close your eyes, _ ay-yo-yo. _ Go to sleep my lit-tle one, _ ay-yo-yo.

- Listen for the flute in this piece.

 "Irlandaise," from *Suite for Flute and Jazz Piano* by Claude Bolling

56

HIGH C AND E ON THE RECORDER

- Review the pitches and fingerings that you know.

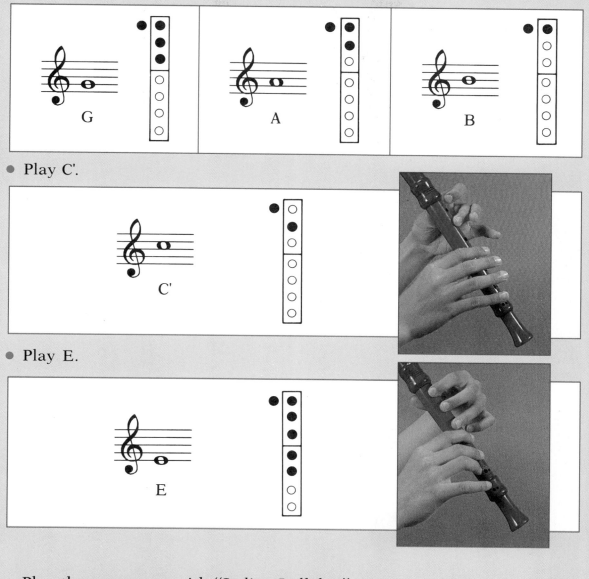

- Play C'.

- Play E.

- Play these patterns with "Indian Lullaby."

- Play the steady beat softly on a drum.

Zuni Indians have lived on the plains of northwestern New Mexico for hundreds of years. The members of the Zuni tribe use symbols from nature for their musical alphabet.

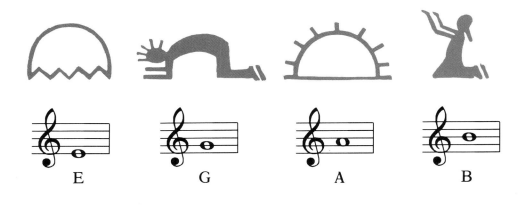

E   G   A   B

- Figure out these melodies by matching each symbol with a letter name.
- Play the melodies on recorder or bells. Where have you heard them before?

- Give the letter names of the pitches in the first measure.

Does this measure repeat?

The Eagle

Music by Hap Palmer
Words by Martha Palmer

1. Born for a west - ern sky, __ sweep - ing a cir - cle
2. Brave and a hunt - er's son, __ the land was his 'til he
3. There on a moun - tain high, _ wound - ed ___ ea - gle
4. Dream - ing of days gone by, __ when In - dian chil - dren

as he flies. _
met a gun. _ He was free _____ when they let him be. _
wants to die. _
watched him fly. _

In a land with-out a friend, __

__ will there be an emp - ty sky ___ where the

D.S. 𝄋 *(verses 3 & 4) al Coda*
to Coda ⊕

ea - gle used to fly ___ in the wind? _____

⊕ *Coda*

Born for a west-ern sky, ___ sweep-ing a cir-cle

as he flies. ___ He was free _____ when they let him be. ___

_____ He was free _____

when they let him be. _____

RHYTHM PATTERNS

At the Grand Canyon in Arizona, visitors can ride burros down the narrow trails to the bottom of the canyon. "On the Trail" is music which can help you to picture a little burro as it moves along—sometimes slowly, sometimes very fast. The rhythms used in "On the Trail" are like the Western rhythms on page 51.

- Clap and say the rhythms below.

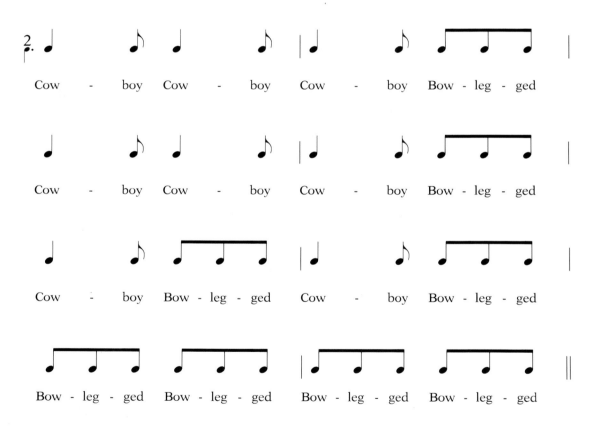

- Say these rhythms with "On the Trail."
- Listen for woodwinds in "On the Trail."

 "On the Trail," from *Grand Canyon Suite,* by Ferde Grofé

In the picture *Wagon Boss* the cowboy stands out. In this quiet scene he is almost like a solo.

- Listen to "On the Trail" again. What solo instruments do you hear? Do you hear any solo instruments against a background of other instruments?
- Which of these are probably "solo" activities? Which are probably group activities?

  collecting stamps

  going camping

  playing baseball

  reading a book

This painting, *Wagon Boss,* is by Charles Russell. He used oil paints to create this picture of a cowboy. Mountains in the background give a feeling of the great open spaces of the American West.

● Pat the beat as you sing this song.

Hani Kouni

Words and music by Jos Wuytack

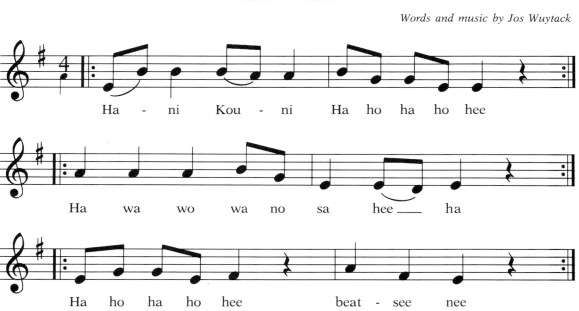

Ha - ni Kou - ni Ha ho ha ho hee

Ha wa wo wa no sa hee ___ ha

Ha ho ha ho hee beat - see nee

RHYTHM EVERYWHERE

● Feel the freedom of the rhythm as you read this poem.

Eagle Flight
An eagle wings gracefully
through the sky.
On the earth I stand
and watch.
My heart flies with it.
—*Alonzo Lopez*

TAKE ANOTHER LOOK

Soaring

- Cloudburst

Hani Kouni

Night Herding Song

- On the Trail

Indian Lullaby

Canoe Song

- Irlandaise

Do you remember?

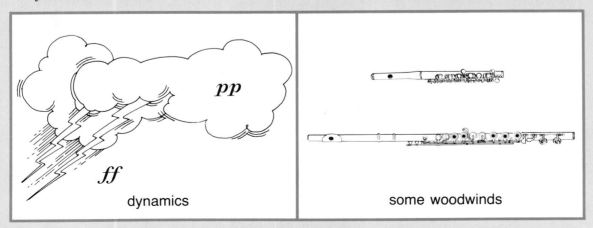

pp

ff

dynamics

some woodwinds

66

JUST CHECKING

1. Find the picture of the flute and piccolo.

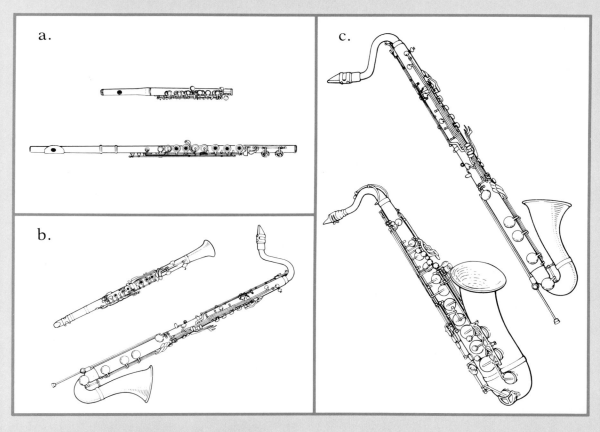

2. Find the symbol for very loud.

   a. *pp*   b. *ff*

3. Find the word which means very soft.

   a. *pianissimo*   b. *fortissimo*

4. Name the pitches.

UNIT 4

SOUNDS OF THE SEASON

Christmas Is Coming

English Folk Song

Christ - mas is com - ing, the goose is get - ting fat.

Please to put a pen - ny in an old man's — hat.

Please to put a pen - ny in an old man's hat.

TEMPO CHANGES

Tempo is the speed of the beat.

- Tap the beat as you listen. Decide if the tempo of this song changes in any way.

O Hanukah

Jewish Folk Song

O Ha - nu - kah, O Ha - nu - kah, come light the me - no - rah!

Let's have a par - ty, we'll all dance the ho - ra.

Gath - er round the ta - ble, we'll give you a treat,

Spin-ning tops to play with, and good things to eat.

And while we are play-ing, the can-dles are burn-ing _ low.

One for each night, they _ shed a sweet light

1.
to re-mind us of days long a-go.

2.
mind us of days long a-go.

Accelerando (ä-chel-ə-rän′dō) is the musical term for gradually getting faster.

- Tap the beat as you listen for *accelerando* in "Russian Dance."

"Russian Dance" ("Trepak"), from *The Nutcracker,* by Peter Ilyich Tchaikovsky

Ritard (ri-tärd′) is the musical term for gradually getting slower.

- Tell how the tempo changes in this song.

Cornish Wassail

English Folk Song

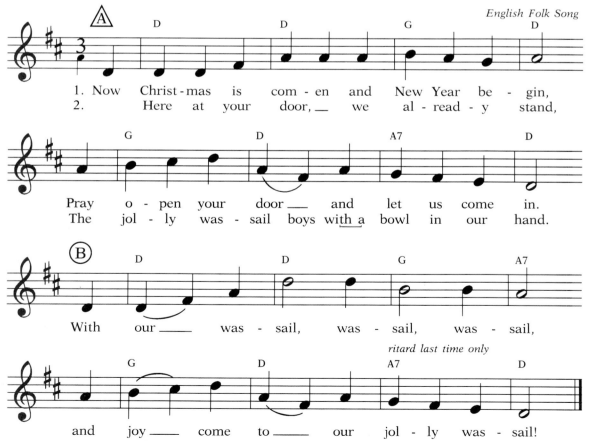

1. Now Christ-mas is com-en and New Year be - gin,
2. Here at your door,__ we al - read - y stand,

Pray o - pen your door __ and let us come in.
The jol - ly was - sail boys with a bowl in our hand.

With our __ was - sail, was - sail, was - sail,

ritard last time only

and joy __ come to __ our jol - ly was - sail!

Christmas Trio, Norman Rockwell, © 1928 courtesy of The Estate of Norman Rockwell

This painting is called *Christmas Trio* and is by Norman Rockwell
(1894–1978). It was used as the front cover illustration for the
December 8, 1923, edition of *The Saturday Evening Post* magazine.

OBOE AND BASSOON

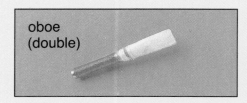

oboe
(double)

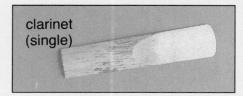

clarinet
(single)

The oboe and bassoon
are woodwind instruments
with double reeds. The
player blows air through
the opening at the end
of the double reed,
which vibrates to
produce a sound.

The oboe is a little more than two feet long. The bassoon
would be nine feet long if it were straightened out.

- Tell how the difference in length makes the two
  instruments sound different from one another.

oboe

bassoon

You will hear the same music played three times. A different group of instruments plays each time.

- As you listen, point to the pictures below to show the instruments you hear.

"Hornpipe," from *Water Music* by George Frederick Handel

COURTESY MUSEUM OF FINE ARTS, Boston: Double Manual Harpsichord. Pieter Jan or Joseph Jan Couchet, Antwerp 1680

• How do the instruments and voices make this song more interesting?

Don Gato

Mexican Folk Song
Words by B.S. and M.S.

1. There once was a cat, Don Ga - to. (Me - ow)
2. Not ev - 'ry - one loved his sing - ing. (Me - ow)

High on a fence sat, Don Ga - to. (Me - ow)
He set neigh - bors' ears a - ring - ing. (Me - ow)

He sang to his love 'neath the moon high a - bove.
One night what a shame, when a neigh - bor took aim,

What a won - der - ful voice, Don Ga - to. _____
And __ struck down Se - ñor Don Ga - to. _____

3. The doctors examined Don Gato.
   They said, "He is dead," poor Don Gato.
   In spite of his voice there was only
   one choice,
   So a funeral was planned for Don Gato.

4. The trip to the cat cemetery
   Was gloomy and not a bit merry.
   A sorrowful end for our talented friend,
   As he took his last trip, Don Gato.

5. There may be a happy ending.
   A miracle seems to be pending.
   With nine lives to spend this is still
   not the end,
   For our wonderful friend, Don Gato.

6. The most that Don Gato could wish for
   Came true as he went by the fish store.
   For when he got there he smelled fish
   in the air,
   And he came back to life, Don Gato.

LOOK FOR FORM

The form of "Zumba, Zumba" is ABA. Why?

Zumba, Zumba

Spanish Folk Song

A

¡Zum-ba, zum-ba! Strike the cym-bal. ¡Zum-ba, zum-ba! Strike the gong!

¡Zum-ba, zum-ba! Beat the tim-bal and the tam-bou-rine and drum!

B

1. Born on this night is a ba-by.
2. What shall I take to the ba-by?

Ev-'ry-one brings him a pre-sent,
What shall I say when I take it?

Brings him a sa-vor-y meat-pie,
I'll bring a gourd for a rat-tle,

Made out of par-tridge and pheas-ant.
I'll ask his moth-er to shake it.

78

● Play a steady beat on one
of these instruments.

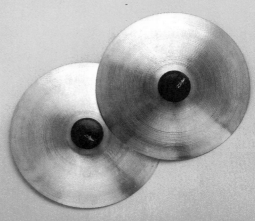

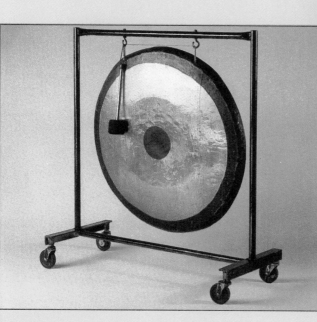

Architects often use some of the same forms as composers.

Which of the forms that you have studied can you see in this building?

The Cathedral of Notre Dame in Paris, France, stands on an island in the Seine River. Building of the cathedral was started in 1163, and the style of the architecture is called Gothic.

The "Dance of the Reed Pipes" is another part of *The Nutcracker* ballet. In the "Dance of the Reed Pipes," the A section is played on three flutes. The form of the "Dance of the Reed Pipes" is

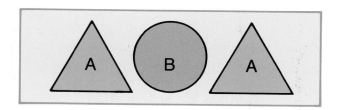

- Listen to the "Dance of the Reed Pipes" and find out how the instruments differ in the B section.
- Raise your hand when you hear section A again.

 "Dance of the Reed Pipes," by Peter Ilyich Tchaikovsky

The form of this song is AABA. Why?

Who Can Retell?

Jewish Folk Song
Arranged By M. Ravina
Words by B.M. Edidin

Ⓐ F   C7   F

Who can re-tell the things that be-fell us? Who can count them?

F   C7   F   B♭   F   *Fine*

In ev-'ry age a he-ro or sage came to our aid!

Ⓑ Cm   G7   Cm

Hark! _____ In days of yore in Is-rael's an-cient land, _____

Fm   G7   Cm

Brave Mac-ca-be-us led the faith-ful band. _____

Fm   G7   Cm

But now all Is-rael must as one a-rise, _____

Fm   G   C7   Fm   *D.C. al Fine*

Re-deem it-self through deed and sac-ri-fice.

82

TELL THE TEXTURE

These pictures show three kinds of textures.

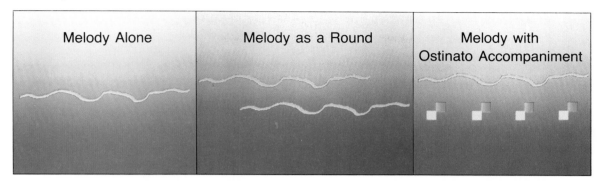

| Melody Alone | Melody as a Round | Melody with Ostinato Accompaniment |

- Match the kind of texture with the music below.

a.

Christ-mas is com-ing, the goose is get-ting fat   Please to put a pen-ny in an

Christ - mas is com-ing,   the

b.

Who can re-tell the   things that be-fell us? Who   can   count   them?

Who can,   who can re - tell   the   tale?   Who can, who can re - tell the tale?

c.

1. There   once   was   a   cat,   Don   Ga - to.   (Me - ow)

DYNAMICS

The musical term for soft is *piano (p).*

The musical term for loud is *forte* (fôr′tā). The symbol for
this word is *f.*

● Find *f* and *p* in this song.

Crescendo (krə-shen′dō) means to get louder gradually. The
symbol for the word is ⟞⟍ .

● Find the *crescendo.*

Deck the Halls

Welsh Folk Song

1. Deck the halls with boughs of hol - ly, Fa la la la la la la la la,

'Tis the sea - son to be jol - ly, Fa la la la la la la la la;

Don we now our gay ap-par-el, Fa la la la la la la la la,

Troll the an-cient Yule-tide car - ol, Fa la la la la la la la la.

2. See the blazing Yule before us,
   Fa la la la la la la la la,
   Strike the harp and join the chorus,
   Fa la la la la la la la la;
   Follow me in merry measure,
   Fa la la la la la la la la,
   While I tell of Yuletide treasure,
   Fa la la la la la la la la.

3. Fast away the old year passes,
   Fa la la la la la la la la,
   Hail the new, ye lads and lasses,
   Fa la la la la la la la la;
   Sing we joyous all together,
   Fa la la la la la la la la,
   Heedless of the wind and weather,
   Fa la la la la la la la la.

The musical term for very soft is **pianissimo (pp).**
The musical term for very loud is **fortissimo (ff).**

● Listen for the different dynamic levels.

"Wolcome Yole!" from *A Ceremony of Carols,*
by Benjamin Britten

- Read "Winter Dark." Use different dynamic levels.

Winter Dark

Winter dark comes early
mixing afternoon
and night.
Soon
there's a comma of a moon,

and each street light
along the
way
puts its period
to the end of day.

Now
a neon sign
punctuates the dark
with a bright
blinking
breathless
exclamation mark!

—*Lilian Moore*

● What dynamic levels do the words of this song suggest?

Almost Day

Words and music by Huddie Ledbetter

1. Chick-en crow-ing for mid-night, __ And it's al-most _ day,
2. Thought I heard __ my moth-er say, _____ It's al-most _ day,

Chick-en crow-ing for mid-night, __ And it's al-most _ day.
Thought I heard __ my moth-er say, _____ It's al-most _ day.

3. Hush and go to sleep now, It's almost day,
   Hush and go to sleep now, It's almost day.

4. Christmas Day is coming, And it's almost day,
   Christmas Day is coming, And it's almost day.

5. Stockings near the fireplace, And it's almost day,
   Stockings near the fireplace, And it's almost day.

6. Chicken crowing for midnight, And it's almost day,
   Chicken crowing for midnight, And it's almost day.

ALMOST DAY
Words and music by Huddie Ledbetter. TRO—© 1951 (renewed 1979) and 1959 Folkways Music Publishers, Inc., New York, N.Y. Used by Permission.

MAJOR AND MINOR

● Play the bells in the order shown.

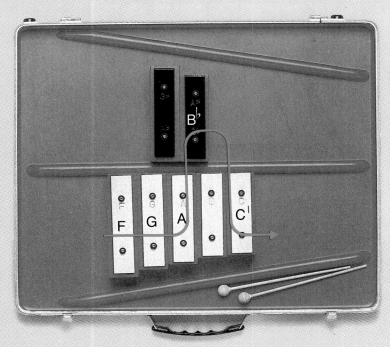

This pattern makes a **major** sound because the half step is between the third and fourth pitches.

● Play the bells in order.

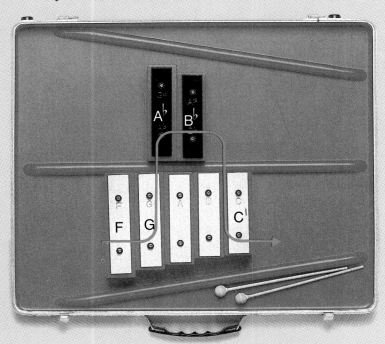

This pattern makes a **minor** sound because the half step is between the second and third pitches.

The form of "Dance of the Reed Pipes" is ABA.

- Listen for the major and minor sections in "Dance of the Reed Pipes," by Tchaikovsky.

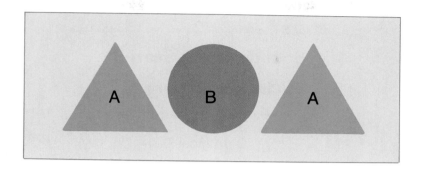

PETER ILYICH
TCHAIKOVSKY

Peter Ilyich Tchaikovsky (pē′tər ēl′yēch chī-kôf′skē) was born in Russia in 1840 and died in 1893. He began piano lessons at the age of four and soon began to compose. When Tchaikovsky was ten, he started law school and later became a clerk in the Ministry of Justice in St. Petersburg. He was not very successful, and he decided to devote his life to music.

Peter Ilyich Tchaikovsky

Tchaikovsky was one of the leading composers of the Romantic period. Some of his famous works include: the ballets *Swan Lake* and *Sleeping Beauty; 1812 Overture;* Fourth, Fifth, and Sixth symphonies; *Romeo and Juliet Overture; Nutcracker Suite.*

TAKE ANOTHER LOOK

Sounds of the Season

Christmas Is Coming

Cornish Wassail ● Hornpipe

Almost Day

● Wolcome Yole!

Deck the Halls

Don Gato O Hanukah ● Russian Dance

Do you remember?

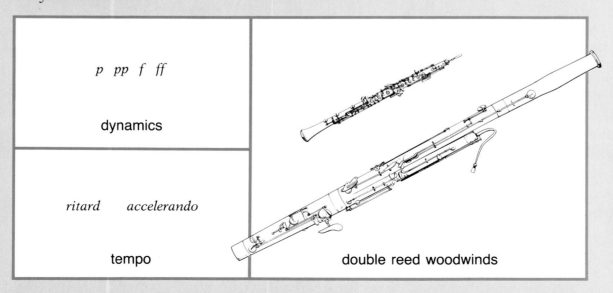

p pp f ff

dynamics

ritard accelerando

tempo   double reed woodwinds

JUST CHECKING

1. Find the picture of the bassoon.

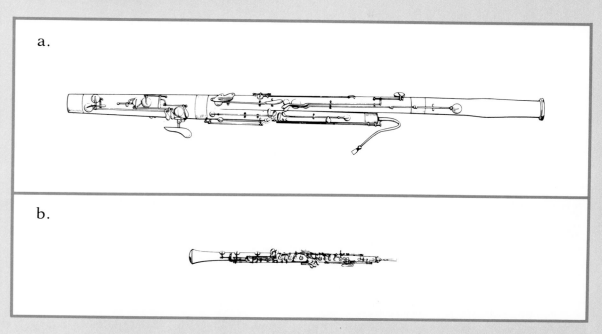

a.

b.

2. Which term means gradually increasing the tempo?
   a. *accelerando*   b. *ritard*

3. Which set of dynamic markings is in the correct order
   from softest to loudest?

   a.   *ff*   *f*   *p*   *pp*

   b.   *pp*   *p*   *f*   *ff*

THE NUTCRACKER

Based on music by Peter Ilyich Tchaikovsky
Production prepared by Erica Whitman Davis

The Nutcracker is an old tale about a little girl's Christmas
Eve in a time long ago, and the nutcracker that she receives
as a present. Our story begins with an **Overture,** which is an
introduction played by the orchestra. The Overture gets us in
the mood for the story. During the Overture, guests arrive for
a wonderful party at Clara's house. Listen and watch as the
curtains open and the magic begins.

 "Overture," from *The Nutcracker,* by Peter Ilyich
Tchaikovsky

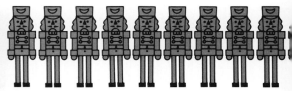

It is the night before Christmas. Clara receives a wonderful present from the mysterious Herr Drosselmeyer. It is a nutcracker in the shape of a soldier.

Clara's brother and his friends are jealous that she got such a wonderful present. They grab the nutcracker and accidentally break it.

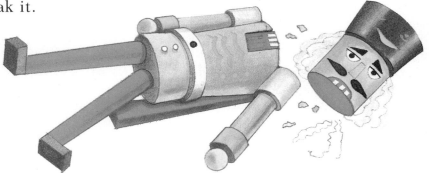

Before she goes to bed, Clara sadly places the nutcracker under the tree. Her father tells her that he will repair it in the morning. But poor Clara can't sleep because she is thinking about her broken nutcracker.

Clara tiptoes back down the stairs to find the nutcracker. There is a strange light around the tree.

As the clock strikes midnight, the room is filled with mysterious shadows. The tree begins to grow taller and taller and the Nutcracker springs to his feet and bows to Clara. Not only does he come to life, but all the toy soldiers come to life too.

Led by the Nutcracker, they march into battle against an invading army of mice.

 "March," from *The Nutcracker*, by Peter Ilyich Tchaikovsky

The battle ends when Clara removes her shoe and throws it at the Mouse King. The mice run away, and the Nutcracker turns into a handsome prince. To thank Clara, the Prince invites her to the Kingdom of Sweets.

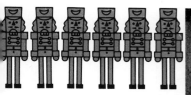
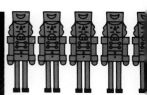

There, the Sugar Plum Fairy welcomes Clara with a dance.

 "Dance of the Sugar Plum Fairy," from *The Nutcracker,* by Peter Ilyich Tchaikovsky

Clara and the Prince join the Sugar Plum Fairy on a beautiful throne. They watch as dancers perform for them. The dancing begins with a group of Russian Cossacks in tall boots and hats.

 "Russian Dance" ("Trepak"), from *The Nutcracker,* by Peter Ilyich Tchaikovsky

The next group of dancers comes from the hot, desert land of Arabia.

 "Arabian Dance," from *The Nutcracker,* by Peter Ilyich Tchaikovsky

Chinese dancers, with their arms hidden in long sleeves, do a dance, bowing and using small steps.

 "Chinese Dance," from *The Nutcracker,* by Peter Ilyich Tchaikovsky

The Sugar Plum Fairy calls for the flowers to waltz. Everyone joins them in the final dance.

 "Waltz of the Flowers," from *The Nutcracker*, by Peter Ilyich Tchaikovsky

At the end, the Sugar Plum Fairy bids Clara farewell. She leaves the Kingdom of Sweets filled with happy thoughts.

UNIT 5

MOUNTAIN MAGIC

New Snow

The pines are white-powdered,
Delicately tossed
With fairy filigrees
Of silver frost.

The top of the mountain
Is lost in a cloud,
While the world is silent
And the wind unloud.

Drink in the beauty,
The shadows...the glow...
The wonder of winter
And the new white snow!

—*Catherine Bryant Rowles*

MELODY AND ACCOMPANIMENT

- Learn the melody. Then sing it as a round.

I Love the Mountains

Traditional

I love the moun - tains, I love the roll - ing hills,

I love the flow - ers, I love the daf - fo - dils;

I love the fire - side when all the lights are low.

Boom - dee - ah - da, Boom - dee - ah - da,

Boom - dee - ah - da, Boom - dee - ah - da.

Sometimes a melody is sung or played alone.

Sometimes it is heard with accompaniment.

Accompaniment is a musical background for the melody.

Collection of Bernard I. Kahn

- Which picture represents melody alone?

- Which represents melody with accompaniment?

- Read this poem in rhythm.

A Wise Old Owl

A wise old owl sat in an oak,
The more he saw the less he spoke;
The less he spoke the more he heard.
Why aren't we all like that wise old bird?

—*Edward Hersey Richards*

An **ostinato** (äs-tə-nät′ō) is a rhythm or melody pattern that keeps repeating throughout a musical piece.

- Learn this ostinato. Say the words as you pat or clap this rhythm. Then pat or clap the rhythm with the poem.

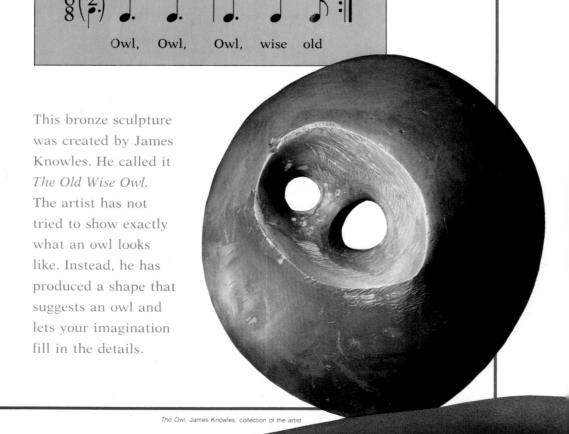

This bronze sculpture was created by James Knowles. He called it *The Old Wise Owl.* The artist has not tried to show exactly what an owl looks like. Instead, he has produced a shape that suggests an owl and lets your imagination fill in the details.

The Owl. James Knowles, collection of the artist

ORFF INSTRUMENTS

Orff instruments are members of the percussion family. They are made of metal and wood. They can be large or small.

You play Orff instruments by striking their tuned bars with mallets. You can play both melodies and accompaniments on Orff instruments. Orff instruments can make up their own special orchestra.

● Look at the Orff instruments. Which ones do you recognize?

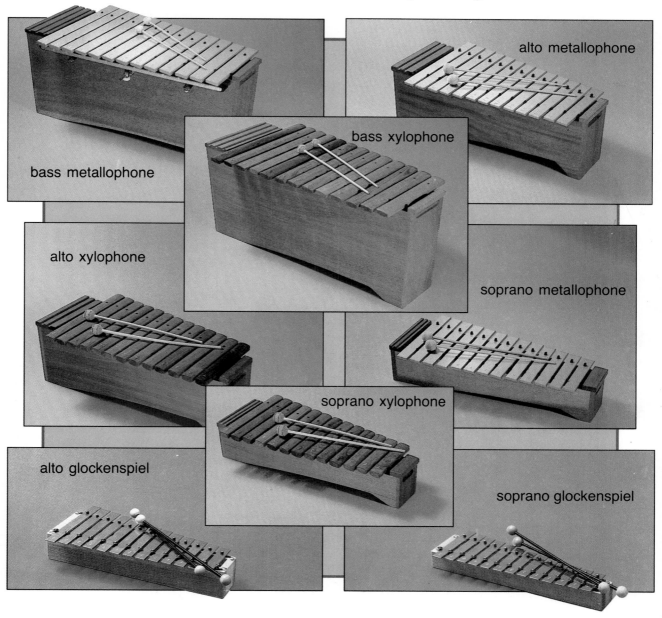

bass metallophone

alto metallophone

bass xylophone

alto xylophone

soprano metallophone

soprano xylophone

alto glockenspiel

soprano glockenspiel

- Move your hand in the air to show the path of the melody.
  What shape did you make?

The Alpine Song

Traditional

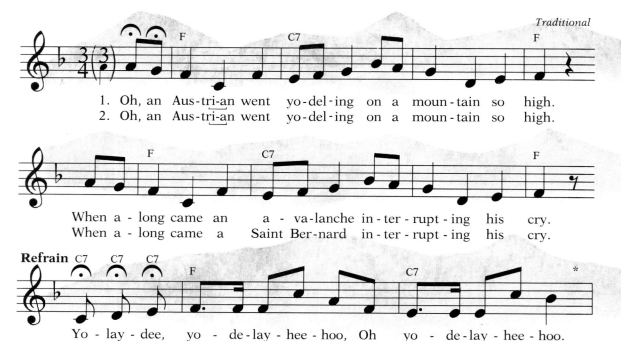

1. Oh, an Aus-tri-an went yo-del-ing on a moun-tain so high.
2. Oh, an Aus-tri-an went yo-del-ing on a moun-tain so high.

When a-long came an a-va-lanche in-ter-rupt-ing his cry.
When a-long came a Saint Ber-nard in-ter-rupt-ing his cry.

Refrain

Yo-lay-dee, yo-de-lay-hee-hoo, Oh yo-de-lay-hee-hoo.

104

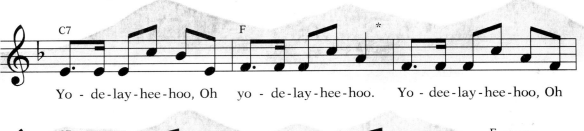

Yo - de - lay - hee - hoo, Oh yo - de - lay - hee - hoo. Yo - dee - lay - hee - hoo, Oh

yo - de - lay - hee - hoo. Yo - de - lay - hee - hoo - oh lay.

1. * shh-shh . . .

2. * pant-pant, shh-shh . . .

3. Oh, an Austrian went yodeling on a mountain so high.
When along came a Guernsey Cow interrupting his cry.
* moo-moo, pant-pant, shh-shh . . .

4. Oh, an Austrian went yodeling on a mountain so high.
When along came a Martian interrupting his cry.
* beep-beep, moo-moo, pant-pant, shh-shh . . .

METER

There is a meter signature at the beginning of each song. The top number tells how many beats are in each measure. The note or number on the bottom tells what kind of note equals one beat.

- Find the meter signature in "Ahrirang." How many beats are there in each measure? What kind of note equals one beat?
- Tap a steady beat with this song.

Ahrirang

Korean Folk Song
English words by M.S.

Ah - ri-rang, Ah - ri-rang, Ah - ra - ri - yo, _____

Walk - ing o - ver roll-ing hills _ of ___ Ah - ri - rang.
Time goes ver - y slow-ly far a - way from Ah - ri - rang.

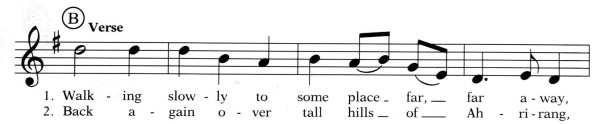

1. Walk - ing slow - ly to some place _ far, __ far a - way,
2. Back a - gain o - ver tall hills _ of ___ Ah - ri - rang,

Hop - ing to re - turn a - gain to Ah - ri - rang ___ some day.
Once a - gain re - turn - ing home _ to ___ Ah - ri - rang.

106

Mountain Retreat and Waterfall (Ch'ing Dynasty), K'un-ts'an

Chinese artist K'un-ts'an painted this landscape called *Mountain Retreat and Waterfall*. K'un-ts'an lived in the seventeenth century. Since Chinese painting grew out of the art of fine handwriting, brush and black ink are often used in creating a picture.

107

- Find the meter signature on this page. How many beats are there in each measure? What kind of note equals one beat?

HOOPSTER

by Biff Fink

When I grow up, I'll be so tall I'll get me a schol-ar- ship for bas- ket ball. And if my head hits the sky I'll get me a gig as a weath-er - eye on T. V. un- der lights work- ing nights that's me grow- ing up out of sight!

D ON THE RECORDER

- Play D on your recorder.

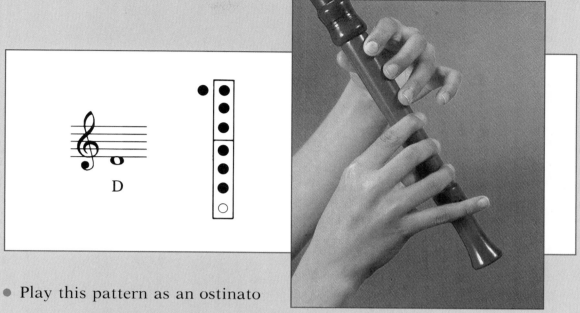

- Play this pattern as an ostinato accompaniment to the A section of "Ahrirang."

This is a **quarter rest** (𝄽). It stands for one beat of silence.

THREE MELODIES IN HARMONY

Sometimes two or more melodies can be combined to make **harmony.**

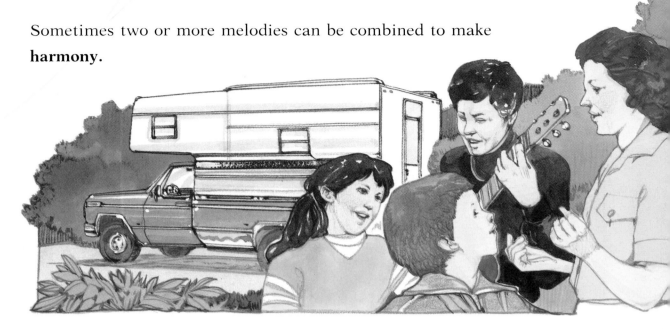

- Listen to each melody alone. Then listen to them sung together.

Going Camping

Words and music by Ray Charles

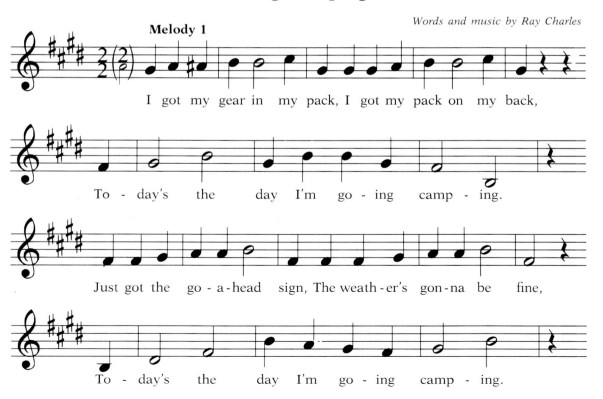

Melody 1

I got my gear in my pack, I got my pack on my back,

To - day's the day I'm go - ing camp - ing.

Just got the go - a - head sign, The weath - er's gon - na be fine,

To - day's the day I'm go - ing camp - ing.

I'm gon-na pitch me a tent, Won't have to pay an - y rent,

It looks like ev - 'ry - thing is "A - O - K."

As far as I can see I think it's gon - na be

A per - fect camp - ing day. _____

Melody 2

The trees and an - i - mals and clear blue skies,

A wa-ter-fall come tum-bling right be-fore my eyes,

Birds that fly a-bove a moun-tain stream,

It's ab-so-lute-ly per-fect, bet-ter than a dream.

Peace and qui-et where the Good Lord smiled,

Fields and fields of flow-ers grow-ing wild,

This is just where I be-long,

I'm Moth-er Na-ture's child. _____

Melody 3

It's time to hit the trail, To hit the hill and dale,

Oh, I love hik-ing in the moun-tains. _____

112

It's great to reach the snow and see the world be - low,

Oh, I love hik - ing in the moun - tains. ____

Each time we stop to eat, We get to rest our feet,

And we'll make it if we take it slow, _____

'Cause the best way to climb Is one step at a time,

And hik - ing is the on - ly way to go. _____

- Do the "1-2-3 Something" (walk, walk, walk, another movement) pattern with "March Past of the Kitchen Utensils." Will this pattern go with the entire piece?

 "March Past of the Kitchen Utensils," by Ralph Vaughan Williams

PLAY A NEW PITCH

- Listen to the song and tap the rhythm of the words "tap on your drum."
- Play the rhythm of the words on a drum as you sing.

Tap on Your Drum

Words and music by Gerald Dyke

Tap on your drum, A-mi-go, tap on your drum.

Tap on your drum, A-mi-go, tap on your drum. You can

tap with your fin-gers, you can tap with your toes.

Tap out a rhy-thm, ni-ño, show how it goes.

These are the pitches you know and one you may not know.

- What is the letter name of the pitch between E and G?

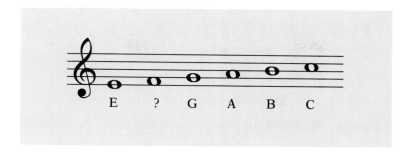

This is where the pitches are located on a keyboard.

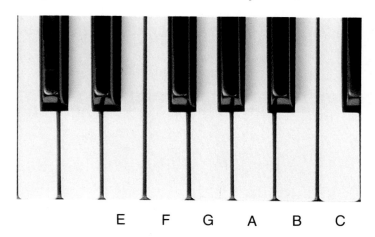

E F G A B C

- Use bells or a keyboard. Practice this pattern that uses just two pitches. Then play it with the song "Tap on Your Drum."

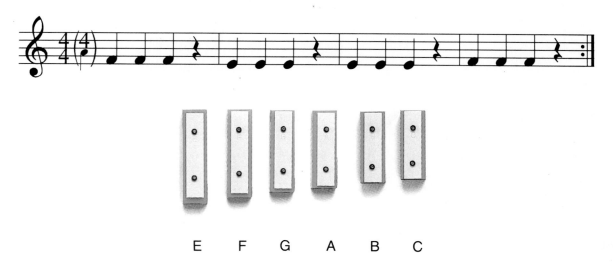

E F G A B C

THE ESKIMO TRADITIONS AND MUSIC

Life in Alaska is difficult. Summer is short, and winter is long, cold, and dark. Many hours are spent finding food and shelter. Music is a way to record history and preserve the traditions of Alaskan culture.

Eskimos made up songs, poems, and chants while they worked. Music helped them pass the time. It also was a way for them to keep their history alive.

These are examples of Eskimo art. The picture to the left is of a reindeer carved from bone. The picture above is an Eskimo stone figure of a woman thinking of a wild goose.

Most Eskimo chants and songs are performed with drumming and movement.

Eskimo *songs* often have short phrases which are repeated many times. Sometimes a song lasts for several hours. A dance song is first sung with syllables that have no meaning. Then it is sung with the words. When older Eskimos sing, they use a sharp, nasal tone color.

Eskimo *drums* were called frame drums. They were made of walrus skin stretched over a large hoop. When they were hit with a curved whale bone or stick, they produced a very low sound. Frame drums are not made any more because they are too difficult to make, and walrus skin is scarce. The old drums that remain are rarely played because they are valuable and delicate.

Movement or dancing is as important as drumming. The dance movements look simple but are not easy to do. Some of the movements tell a story. Some dances have remained the same for hundreds of years.

- As you listen to "Dance Song," imagine what movements the dancers would use.

 "Dance Song" performed by Leo Kaleak and Group at Point Barrow in 1946

The picture to the left is of a figure carved from sea-washed whalebone. Eskimo carvers use stone, driftwood, bone, and ivory. They frequently carve animal shapes for their children to use as toys. Carvings are also made of whales, walrus, and scenes of daily life.

- How is this song like the Eskimo "Dance Song"?

Eskimo Ice Cream

Inuit Indian Song
Collected by Ben Snowball
and Rita Blumenstein

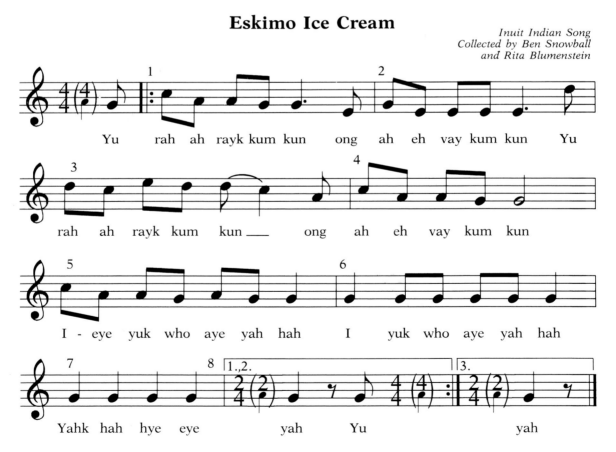

Yu rah ah rayk kum kun ong ah eh vay kum kun Yu

rah ah rayk kum kun ___ ong ah eh vay kum kun

I - eye yuk who aye yah hah I yuk who aye yah hah

Yahk hah hye eye yah Yu yah

• Play this drum part with "Eskimo Ice Cream."

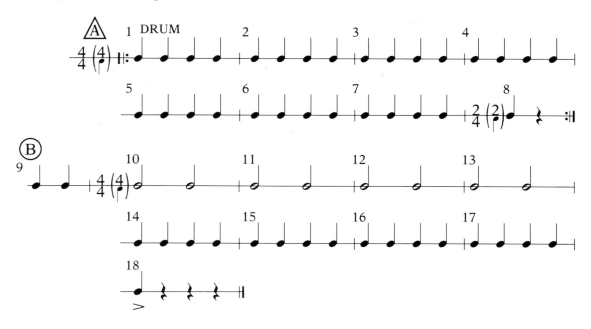

• Do these movements with the B section of "Eskimo Ice Cream."

(measure 9)			(10)		(11)		(12)		(13)	
1	2	1-2	3-4	1-2	3-4	1-2	3-4	1-2	3-4	
stir	stir	stir	lick	lick	put bowl down	pick up parka	put parka on	pick up bowl	put bowl on lap	

	(14)				(15)				(16)			
1	2	3	4	1	2	3	4	1	2	3	4	
walk right hand	walk left hand	walk right hand	walk left hand	dip	serve	dip	serve	dip	serve	lick	lick	

	(17)				(18)			
1	2	3	4	1	2	3	4	
lick	lick	lick	lick	*swallow!!*				

THE PENTATONIC SCALE

A **pentatonic scale** has five different pitches. There are many kinds of pentatonic scales.

The pitches in "Eskimo Ice Cream" make a pentatonic scale.

- Play them on bells.

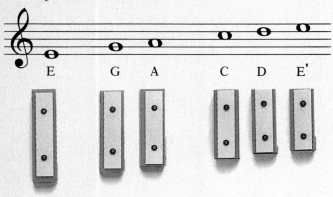

E G A C D E'

- Make up rhythm patterns and play them using these pitches.

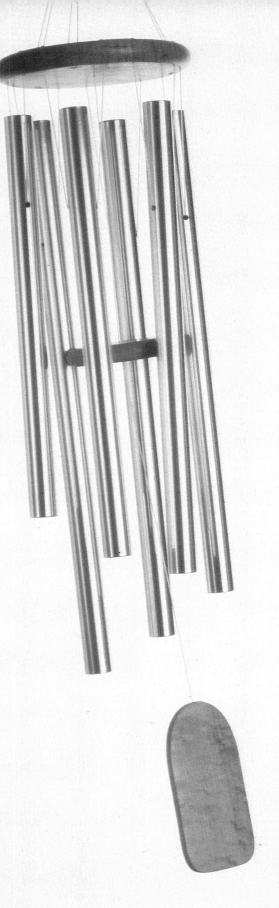

These are pentatonic wind chimes. They were created by musician Garry Kvistad and his wife, Diane. The chimes are made of metal tubes that are cut close to the right length and then tuned to the exact pitches of a pentatonic scale. The sounds they produce when they are shaken by the wind are beautiful and mysterious.

TWO WAYS OF SHOWING METER

Notice the two meter signatures. They both mean that a
quarter note is equal to one beat.

Hill an' Gully

Calypso music from Jamaica
Words by M. S.

2. So I stayed all night there, Hill an' gully
    I could not go anywhere, Hill an' gully.
    But I really didn't even care, Hill an' gully
    As I rode my horse around the square, Hill an' gully.

    Refrain

Mountain ranges have names with interesting rhythms. You can use these rhythms to make a rhythm pattern.

- Clap and say the rhythm of the name of each mountain range.
- Choose two rhythms and say one after the other.
- Combine several names to make a rhythm pattern. Try different combinations until you find a pattern you like.

Rock - y   Moun - tains

Swiss Alps

Him - a - lay - as

Cum - ber - land

Si - er - ra   Ma - dres

122

CREATE A MELODY AND ACCOMPANIMENT

- Follow these steps to create a melody and accompaniment.

  Partner 1 creates the melody by choosing a rhythm and pitches.

1

- Pat your favorite mountain rhythm on your knees.
- Play the mountain rhythm on resonator bells. Use these pitches of a pentatonic scale.

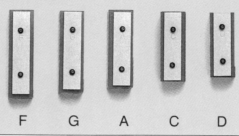

F   G   A   C   D

2 Partner 2 plays this pattern to create an accompaniment.

- Use two pitches from the pentatonic scale.

Moun - tains   of the world

3 Partner 3 creates another accompaniment.

- Play this rhythm on F and C at the same time.

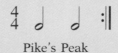

Pike's Peak

- Now play all three parts together. Listen to each other. Try to balance melody and accompaniments.

TAKE ANOTHER LOOK

Mountain Magic

Tap on Your Drum

I Love the Mountains

Hill an' Gully

Going Camping

● March Past of the Kitchen Utensils

The Alpine Song

Do you remember?

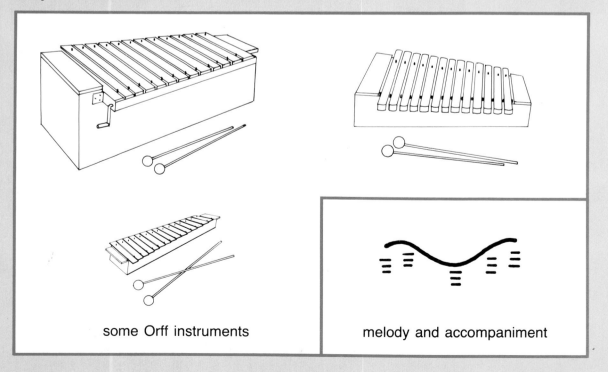

some Orff instruments

melody and accompaniment

JUST CHECKING

1. Which drawing shows melody alone?

   a.    b.

2. Which is an Orff instrument?

   a. violin   b. clarinet   c. soprano metallophone

3. Which is the bass xylophone?

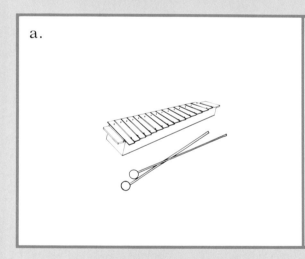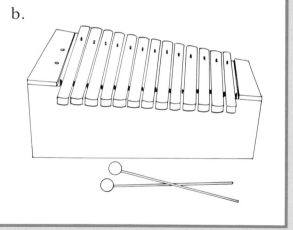

a.

b.

4. Which instrument has the highest sound?

   a. bass metallophone   b. soprano glockenspiel   c. alto xylophone

UNIT 6

LET US SING TOGETHER!

- What do these people have in common?

- What differences would you hear in their voices?

HARMONY

● How can you sing this song to create harmony?

Let Us Sing Together

Czechoslovakian Round

Let us sing to-geth - er, Let us sing to-geth - er, One and all a

joy - ous song. Let us sing to - geth - er, One and all a

joy - ous song. Let us sing a - gain and a - gain,

Let us sing a - gain and a - gain. Let us sing a - gain and a - gain,

One and all a joy - ous song.

When you know this song well, one person can sing the verse and another person can sing the refrain at the same time to produce harmony.

It's a Small World

Words and music by Richard M. Sherman
and Robert B. Sherman

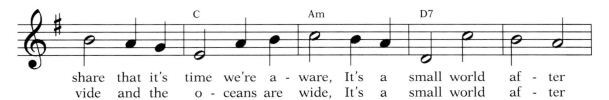

1. It's a world of laugh - ter, a world of tears; it's a
2. There is just one moon and one gol - den sun and a

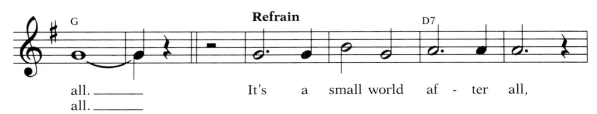

world of hopes and a world of fears. There's so much that we
smile means friend - ship to ev - 'ry - one. Though the moun - tains di -

share that it's time we're a - ware, It's a small world af - ter
vide and the o - ceans are wide, It's a small world af - ter

Refrain

all. _____ It's a small world af - ter all,
all. _____

It's a small world af - ter all. It's a small world

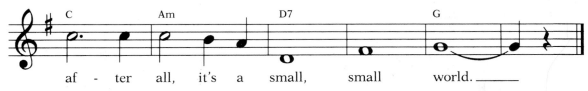

af - ter all, it's a small, small world. _____

IT'S A SMALL WORLD
© 1963 Wonderland Music Co. Inc. Words and Music Richard M. Sherman and
Robert B. Sherman

- Play this rhythm on a tambourine to accompany section A.

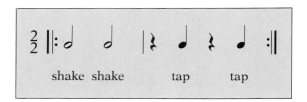

shake shake   tap   tap

- Choose another instrument and make up your own rhythm pattern to accompany section B.

Do, Lord

Spiritual

Do, Lord, Oh Do, Lord, oh do re-mem-ber me,

Do, Lord, Oh Do, Lord, oh do re-mem-ber me.

Do, Lord, Oh Do, Lord, oh do re-mem-ber me, Look a-

A **descant** is a simple melody. It usually has higher pitches than the main melody and makes harmony with it.

- Listen for the harmony created when one group adds this descant to the song.

A Descant for "Do, Lord"

THE STAR-SPANGLED BANNER

In August of 1814 America was at war with Great Britain. The British fleet had attacked Washington, D.C., and burned many important buildings. Then the fleet traveled up the Chesapeake Bay to attack Baltimore at Fort McHenry.

No one at Fort McHenry knew when the enemy would strike, but they prepared for the attack. A special flag was made to fly over the fort. It let the British know that Americans were proud of their country and would fight for it.

Two men watched in a small boat. Francis Scott Key and John Skinner were on their way to the British fleet. They carried a request from President Madison for the release of a prisoner, Dr. William Beanes. As the two Americans came close to the fleet, they raised the white flag of truce. The British officers agreed to let the doctor go free but insisted that all the Americans remain on board until after the battle.

View of Bombardment of Fort McHenry, by John Bower

In September the battle began. There was nothing the three captive Americans could do but watch and hope.

The fighting lasted all day and all night. As the sun began to rise, the American flag was still flying over Fort McHenry. The Americans had won the battle! Francis Scott Key was so happy he took out an old envelope and began to write a poem about how he felt.

The *Baltimore American* newspaper published the poem. It was so well liked that it was run off on handbills, and people put the words to a popular tune of the day. It became one of the most widely sung patriotic songs ever written.

On March 3, 1931, President Herbert Hoover signed a bill making "The Star-Spangled Banner" the American national anthem. Francis Scott Key would have been surprised and proud to know that the poem he had written on that morning of American victory would one day become the national anthem of our country.

By Dawn's Early Light (detail). Edward Percy Moran

This engraving was copied from the painting *By Dawn's Early Light,* by Edward Percy Moran. It shows Francis Scott Key observing Fort McHenry from aboard ship.

Francis Scott Key

● Why do we stand when this song is played or sung?

This 19-star flag with the belt-buckle formation was used in 1817 and included Indiana as the 19th state. It was an unofficial flag.

This flag was carried by the West Virginia Cavalry Unit during the Civil War.

The Star-Spangled Banner

Music attributed to J. S. Smith
Words by Francis Scott Key

1. Oh, __ say! can you see, by the dawn's ear - ly light,
2. On the shore, dim - ly seen thro' the mists of the deep,
3. Oh, __ thus be it ev-er when __ free men shall stand

What so proud - ly we hailed at the twi-light's last gleam - ing?
Where the foe's haugh - ty host in dread si - lence re - pos - es,
Be - tween their loved homes and the war's des - o - la - tion!

Whose broad stripes and bright stars, through the per - il - ous fight,
What is that which the breeze, o'er the tow - er - ing steep,
Blest with vic - t'ry and peace, may the heav'n res - cued land

O'er the ram - parts we watched were so gal - lant - ly stream - ing?
As it fit - ful - ly blows, half con - ceals, half dis - clos - es?
Praise the Pow'r that hath made and pre - served us a na - tion.

134

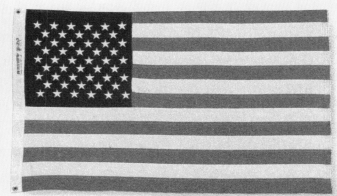

The comet-pattern flag was the official flag from July 4, 1845 until July 4, 1846. It included Florida as the 27th state.

This flag has been the official flag since 1960 when Hawaii joined the Union.

And the rock - ets' red glare, the bombs burst - ing in air,
Now it catch - es the gleam of the morn - ing's first beam,
Then __ con - quer we must, for our cause it is just,

Gave proof through the night that our flag was still there.
In full glo - ry re - flect-ed now __ shines on the stream;
And this be our mot-to "In __ God is our trust."

Oh, say, does that __ Star-Span-gled Ban - ner __ yet __ wave __
'Tis the Star-Span - gled __ Ban - ner, oh, long may __ it __ wave __
And the Star-Span - gled __ Ban - ner, in tri - umph __ shall __ wave __

O'er the land __ of the free and the home of the brave?
O'er the land __ of the free and the home of the brave!
O'er the land __ of the free and the home of the brave!

A conductor can show musicians how loudly or softly to play by the size of his or her conducting pattern. The conductor usually makes a smaller pattern for softer music and a larger pattern for louder music.

The word *mezzo* (met'sō) means medium. In the "National Emblem March" the music is sometimes **mezzo piano** (medium soft) and sometimes **mezzo forte** (medium loud).

very soft	soft	medium soft	medium loud	loud	very loud
pianissimo	*piano*	*mezzo piano*	*mezzo forte*	*forte*	*fortissimo*
pp	*p*	*mp*	*mf*	*f*	*ff*

- Conduct the "National Emblem March" with the recording. Follow this pattern. Show the contrast in dynamics by changing the size of your conducting pattern.

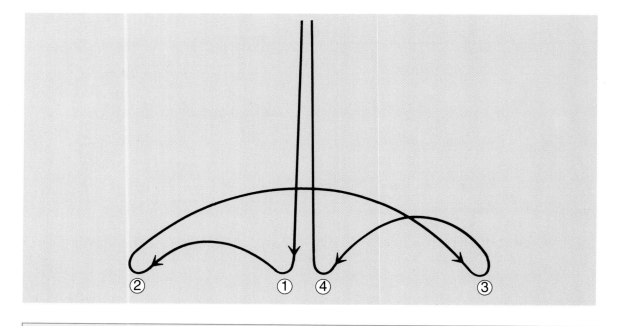

 "National Emblem March," by Edwin Bagley

- Is the conducting pattern for the "National Emblem March" the correct one for this song?

Join Hands in Brotherhood

German Folk Song
Words by B.S.

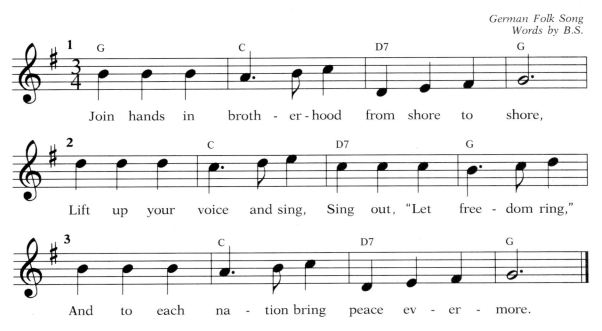

1 Join hands in broth-er-hood from shore to shore,

2 Lift up your voice and sing, Sing out, "Let free-dom ring,"

3 And to each na-tion bring peace ev-er-more.

MORE HARMONY

- Play a steady beat on the pitches F and C throughout this song. Use resonator bells, bell chimes, or keyboard instruments.

Mr. Frog Went Courtin'

American Folk Song

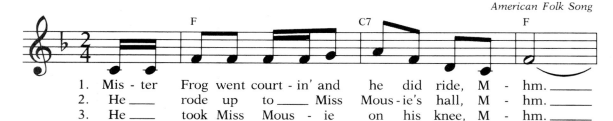

1. Mis - ter Frog went court - in' and he did ride, M - hm. _____
2. He ____ rode up to ____ Miss Mous - ie's hall, M - hm. _____
3. He ____ took Miss Mous - ie on his knee, M - hm. _____

— Mis - ter Frog went court - in' and he did ride,
— He ____ rode up to ____ Miss Mous - ie's hall, He
— He ____ took Miss Mous - ie on his knee, He

Sword and pis - tol by his side, M - hm. _____
gave a loud knock and he gave a loud call, M - hm. _____
said, "Miss Mouse, will you mar - ry me?" M - hm. _____

4. Miss Mousie blushed and hung her head, M-hm.
   Miss Mousie blushed and hung her head,
   "You'll have to ask Uncle Rat," she said, M-hm.

5. Next day Uncle Rat he rode to town, M-hm.
   Next day Uncle Rat he rode to town,
   To get his niece a wedding gown, M-hm.

138

A **chord** is a combination of three or more pitches sounded together. The letters above the staff show what chords to play. The **chord root** or lowest pitch of the chord gives the chord its name.

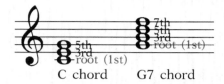

C chord   G7 chord

- Which chords are used in this song?

You can sing a harmony part for "Love Somebody" by singing the chord root C or G.

Love Somebody

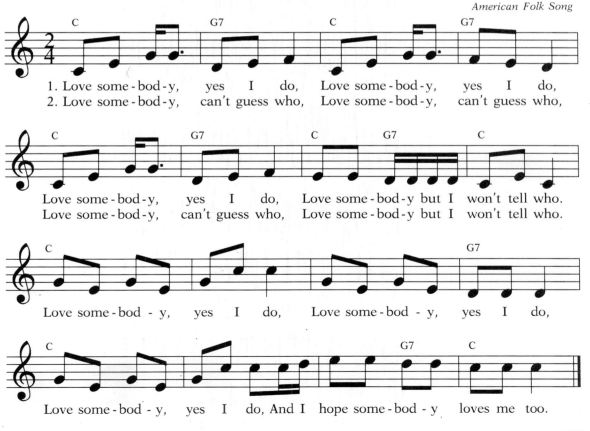

American Folk Song

1. Love some-bod-y, yes I do, Love some-bod-y, yes I do,
2. Love some-bod-y, can't guess who, Love some-bod-y, can't guess who,

Love some-bod-y, yes I do, Love some-bod-y but I won't tell who.
Love some-bod-y, can't guess who, Love some-bod-y but I won't tell who.

Love some-bod-y, yes I do, Love some-bod-y, yes I do,

Love some-bod-y, yes I do, And I hope some-bod-y loves me too.

139

VALENTINE PUZZLES

- Name the notes in each staff to complete the words and find the secret message.

1. You'r [] my f [] vorit []

V [] l [] ntin [] .

2. [] oo [] fri [] n [] s

[] r [] [] st.

3. Musi [] [] l

[] r [] [] tin [] s to [] ll!

In the descant for "Mr. Frog Went Courtin'" there are two ties (‿). A **tie** means hold the sound for the length of both notes.

● Play these descants on the recorder or bells.

Mr. Frog Went Courtin'

Love Somebody

COMPOSE YOURSELF!

Differences in tempos and dynamic levels make music interesting.

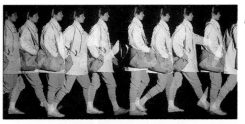
lento
(slow)

allegro
(fast, lively)

presto
(very fast)

- Say your name in each tempo.
- Pat the beat as you listen to this song.
- How does the tempo change?

Al Citron

Latin American Stone-passing Game

Al ci - tron de un fan - dan - go, san - go, san - go, sa - ba - ré.

Sa - ba - ré de la ron - de - la con su tri - ki, tri - ki trón.

142

● Say your name in different dynamic levels.

very soft *pianissimo* *pp*	soft *piano* *p*	medium soft *mezzo piano* *mp*
medium loud *mezzo forte* *mf*	loud *forte* *f*	very loud *fortissimo* *ff*

● Listen for different tempos and dynamic levels.

 "It Don't Mean a Thing If It Ain't Got That Swing,"
by Duke Ellington

JAZZ, AN AMERICAN STYLE

Jazz is American music. It began in New Orleans around
1900 when the musicians began to use the rhythms of African
drummers in their own music. Jazz is a mixture of many
different styles of American music, including ragtime, blues,
boogie-woogie, and gospel music.

In jazz, the musicians **improvise.** This means that they take a
melody and change it as they are playing or singing. They
express what they feel at the moment the music is being
performed.

- Use the melody of the B section of "Do, Lord" as your
  theme. Sing or play it "your way" by changing the rhythm
  and pitches.

A jazz band playing in a New Orleans club

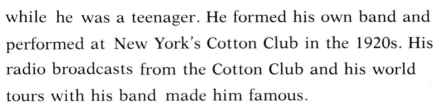

EDWARD KENNEDY "DUKE" ELLINGTON

Duke Ellington (1899–1974) was an American pianist and orchestra leader, and one of the greatest composers in jazz history. He was born in Washington, D.C., and started his musical career there while he was a teenager. He formed his own band and performed at New York's Cotton Club in the 1920s. His radio broadcasts from the Cotton Club and his world tours with his band made him famous.

Duke Ellington's music had a special style that made it stand out from others at that time. Even though his music was much more complicated than people were used to hearing, many of his pieces became very popular. He composed songs and short pieces for his band, wrote music for the theater and movies, and composed religious music and longer concert pieces. Duke Ellington won many awards and honors in his lifetime, and was one of America's greatest musicians.

TAKE ANOTHER LOOK

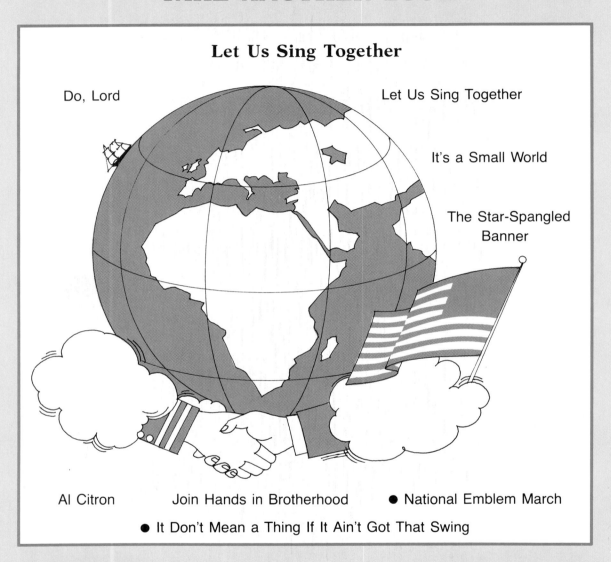

Let Us Sing Together

Do, Lord

Let Us Sing Together

It's a Small World

The Star-Spangled Banner

Al Citron

Join Hands in Brotherhood

● National Emblem March

● It Don't Mean a Thing If It Ain't Got That Swing

Do you remember?

mp *mf*	*lento* *allegro* *presto*
dynamics	tempo

JUST CHECKING

1. Which word does not name tempo?

   a. *presto*   b. *lento*

   c. *mezzo*   d. *allegro*

2. Which word means slow?

   a. *presto*   b. *allegro*   c. *lento*

3. Which word means very fast?

   a. *mezzo*   b. *presto*   c. *lento*

4. Which word or words mean medium soft?

   a. *presto*   b. *mezzo piano*

   c. *mezzo forte*   d. *forte*

5. Which of the following is the dynamic marking for *mezzo piano*?

   mp   *p*   *f*   *mf*

6. Which of the following is the dynamic marking for *mezzo forte*?

   f   *mp*   *p*   *mf*

7. Which is louder?

   mf   *mp*

THE STONECUTTER

A musical play based on a Japanese folk tale
by Randy DeLelles and Jeff Kriske

> **Cast:**
>
> Narrator
>
> Tasuka, the stonecutter
>
> Prince, Musicians, and Dancers (approximately 8–12)
>
> Cherry Blossom Dancers (6–8)
>
> Cloud Children (4)
>
> Choir
>
> Instrument Players

Look into the Rose

© DeLelles/Kriske

Look in-to the rose, ___ look in-to the rose ___ for the beau-ty ___ of the earth lies in one pe-tal.

Once upon a time there lived a lowly stonecutter named Tasuka. Each day, for miles around, you could hear the sound of his hammer and chisel as he chipped away at the base of a great mountain.

The Stonecutter at Work

© DeLelles/Kriske

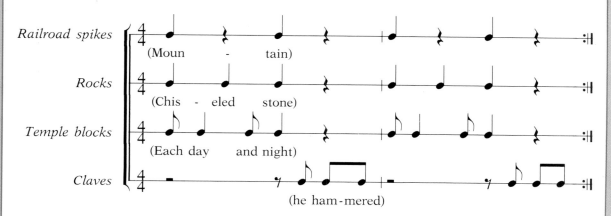

Railroad spikes — (Moun - tain)

Rocks — (Chis - eled stone)

Temple blocks — (Each day and night)

Claves — (he ham-mered)

Tasuka was content with his life and asked for nothing more. This pleased the great spirit who lived within the mountain.

Spirit Motif

All instruments

(Glissando on wind chimes)

One morning, as Tasuka worked, a magnificent procession passed by. A royal prince, clothed in splendid robes, led a group of musicians and dancers. Tasuka watched.

Procession

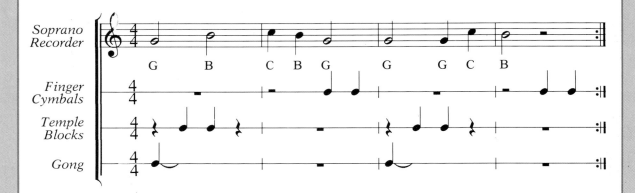

Tasuka stood silently until the procession passed out of sight. "If only I could be a prince," he thought. The great spirit heard him and granted Tasuka his wish. (Repeat the "Spirit Motif.")

Tasuka was very pleased to become a prince. He enjoyed his newfound wealth and life of ease. Each morning he sat in his garden among the beautiful flowers and blossoms.

Sakura

Japanese Folk Song
Arranged by DeLelles/Kriske

Sa - ku - ra, Sa - ku - ra, Ya - yo - i - no - so - ra - wa,

Mi - wa - ta - su - ka - gi - ri - ka - su - mi - ka - ku - mo - ka.

Ni - o - i - zo, i - zu - ru. I - za - ya, I - za - ya,

Mi - ni - yu - kan.

But the afternoon sun withered the blossoms. ("Sun Motif")

Sun Motif

Tasuka felt the strength of the sun. "If only I could be the sun," he thought. The great spirit heard him and granted Tasuka his wish. (Repeat the "Spirit Motif.")

Tasuka was very pleased to be the sun. And to show his great power, he burned the fields and scorched the land. He created a great drought. (Repeat the "Sun Motif.")

The people prayed for rain. And soon a cloud came and covered the sun. ("Cloud Motif")

Cloud Motif

R.D./J.K.

Tasuka saw the power of the cloud.
"If only I were a cloud," he thought.
The great spirit heard him and once
again granted Tasuka his wish.
(Repeat the "Spirit Motif.")

Tasuka was pleased to be the cloud. With this new power he could create rain. But he was not satisfied with the gentle rain. He caused furious storms. Tasuka enjoyed making the skies flash with lightning and crash with thunder. Soon rivers overflowed and villages were destroyed and washed away.

But the great mountain remained. Tasuka saw the mountain's strength and wished, "If only I could be a mountain." The spirit heard him and granted his wish. But then the spirit departed. (Repeat the "Spirit Motif.")

Tasuka was pleased to be the great mountain. Now he was greater and more powerful than the prince, the sun, and the cloud. But one day, Tasuka stopped to listen. (pause) He heard the faint sound of a hammer and chisel at his feet. (Repeat "The Stonecutter at Work.")

Tasuka realized the mountain was not the most powerful . . . and he trembled. (Repeat "Look into the Rose.")

155

UNIT 7 SPRING VARIATIONS

And Suddenly Spring

The winds of March were sleeping.
I hardly felt a thing.
The trees were standing quietly.
It didn't seem like spring.
Then suddenly the winds awoke
And raced across the sky.
They bumped right into April,
Splashing springtime in my eye.
—*Margaret Hillert*

SAY "WELCOME" MANY WAYS

● Sing the A section. Say the words of the B section in rhythm
  as you do the action shown. Sing the A section again.

Funga Alafia

Liberian Welcome Dance

Fun-ga A - la - fia Ah-shay Ah-shay Fun-ga A - la - fia Ah-shay Ah-shay

With my   I   with my   I   with my   I   See? I have
brains   welcome   words   welcome   heart   welcome   nothing up
          you   you   you   my sleeve

With my brains   I welcome you   with my words   I welcome you

with my heart   I welcome you   See? I have nothing
                                            up my sleeve

158

A **variation** is a change in the music that still keeps the original idea. Variations can be made in rhythm, form, melody, and other musical elements.

- Think of ways to vary, or change, the way you walk. Then play the variation game. Every time you hear "change," walk a different way.
- Listen for the variations of a familiar melody.

Variations on "Ah, vous dirai-je, Maman" (excerpt), by Wolfgang Amadeus Mozart

LETTER NAMES

Each line and space on the staff has its own letter name. The musical alphabet uses only the letters from A to G. Voices and instruments produce pitches which can be identified by these letter names.

● Play the pitch of each note. First play the pitches from bottom to top (upward) and from top to bottom (downward). Then play the pitches in any order.

- Find the words "Look out, look out!" in this song. What are the letter names of the notes for these words?

Scotland's Burning

Traditional

Scot-land's burn-ing, Scot-land's burn-ing! Look out, look out!

Fire! Fire! Fire! Fire! Pour on wa - ter, pour on wa - ter!

- Make up a different movement for each two measures of this song.

METER SIGNATURE

The meter signature tells how beats are grouped. The top number tells how many beats are in a measure. The bottom number tells what kind of note is equal to one beat. If the bottom number is 4, the quarter note is equal to one beat. If the bottom number is 8, the eighth note is equal to one beat.

- Tell which note is equal to one beat in each meter signature. $\frac{4}{4}$ $\frac{6}{8}$ $\frac{3}{4}$ $\frac{2}{4}$
- Say this poem with a feeling of 2 beats per measure. Then say it again with a feeling of 3 beats per measure.

Solomon Grundy

Solomon Grundy,
Born on a Monday,
Christened on Tuesday,
Married on Wednesday,
Took ill on Thursday,
Worse on Friday,
Died on Saturday,
Buried on Sunday,
This is the tale
Of Solomon Grundy.

—*Anonymous*

- Pat the beat in "The Wee Falorie Man." Does this song have a feeling of 2 beats, 3 beats, or 6 beats per measure?
- What does the meter signature mean?

The Wee Falorie Man

Irish Folk Song
Collected by David Hammond

1. I am the wee Fa-lo-rie man,
2. I am a good old work-in' man,

A rat-tlin', rov-in' I-rish-man,
Each day I car-ry my wee tin can,

I can do all that ev-er you can,
A large pen-ny bap and a clipe — of ham,

For I am the wee Fa-lo-rie man.
I am a good old work-in' man.

163

6/8 METER

The meter signature 6/8 shows that there are six beats in a measure and that each eighth note is equal to one beat. You feel the song "The Wee Falorie Man" on page 163 in two (2/♩.) instead of six. This is because you hear the beats grouped into two sets of three beats each.

The meter signature 6/8 is also used for songs that have a feeling of six beats per measure.

● Pat the beat as you listen.

 "Barcarolle," from *Tales of Hoffmann*, by Jacques Offenbach

Il Canal Grande e Palazzo Bembo (detail). Canaletto. WOBURN ABBEY. Collection Duca di Bedford

- Tap each rhythm.

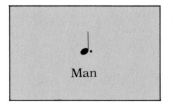

Man

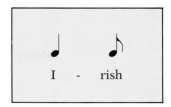

I - rish

I am the

- This is the rhythm pattern for a song you know. Tap it.
- What song is it?

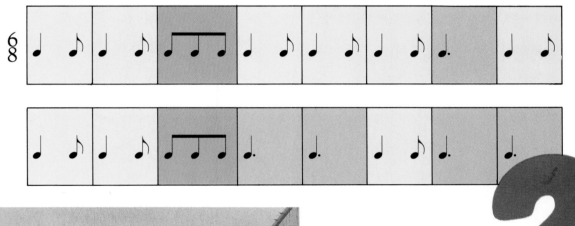

The Grand Canal and Bembo Palace is by the Italian painter Canaletto (1697–1768). Canaletto was born in Venice and used scenes of the city as the subject of many of his works.

SYNCOPATED RHYTHM

- Find this rhythm pattern ♪ ♩ ♪ in "Artsa Alinu." This pattern is a short-long-short pattern. It is called a **syncopated** (sing′kə-pāt-əd) rhythm.
- Clap the syncopated rhythm as you listen to the song.

Artsa Alinu

Hebrew Song

Ar - tsa a - li - nu, Ar - tsa a - li - nu.

Ar - tsa a - li - nu. _____

K'var cha - rash - nu v - gam za - ra _____ nu.

A - val od lo ka tsar nu.

166

- Listen to the "Russian Sailor's Dance." Follow the listening map.

 "Russian Sailor's Dance," from *The Red Poppy*, by Reinhold Glière (rīn′hōlt gli-er′)

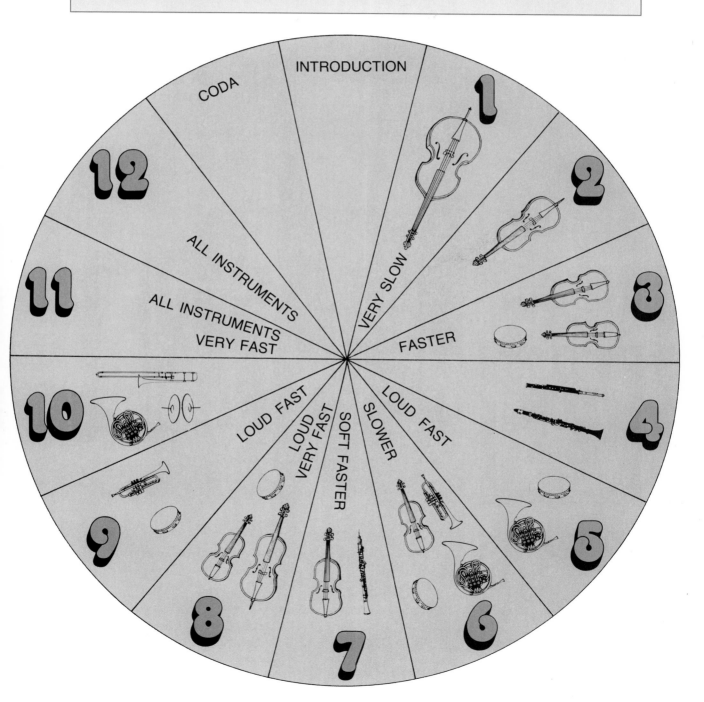

MORE VARIATIONS

A variation is a change or a different form of an idea. Variation helps make paintings, poetry, and music more interesting.

COURTESY THE MUSEUM OF MODERN ART, New York. Herbin, Auguste. *Composition on the Word "Vie,"* 2. 1950. Oil on canvas. 5'7½ x 38¼". The Sidney and Harriet Janis Collection. Gift to the Museum of Modern Art

WHITNEY MUSEUM OF AMERICAN ART. *Gran Cairo.* 1962. Frank Stella.

COURTESY O.K. HARRIS GALLERY, New York. *Aesop #10.* Tony King.

Homage to the Square: Glow. Josef Albers. HIRSHHORN MUSEUM AND SCULPTURE GARDEN, Washington, DC

These paintings show variations using shapes. The large picture, *Composition on the Word "Vie,"* 2, is by Auguste Herbin. At top left is *Gran Cairo,* by Frank Stella, and at bottom left is *Aesop #10,* by Tony King. The final picture is *Homage to the Square: Glow,* by Josef Albers.

In each verse of this poem the same idea is repeated
with variation.

Dream Variations

To fling my arms wide
In some place of the sun,
To whirl and to dance
Till the white day is done.
Then rest at cool evening
Beneath a tall tree
While night comes on gently,
  Dark like me—
That is my dream!

To fling my arms wide
In the face of the sun,
Dance! Whirl! Whirl!
Till the quick day is done.
Rest at pale evening . . .
A tall, slim tree . . .
Night coming tenderly
Black like me.

—*Langston Hughes*

KNOCK AT THE DOOR

- Find this syncopated rhythm pattern in the song. ♪♩ ♪
- Raise your hand each time you hear the flute.

Somebody's Knocking at Your Door

Spiritual

Some - bod - y's knock - ing at your door. _____

Some - bod - y's knock - ing at your door. _____

O _____ sin - ner, why don't you an - swer?

Some - bod - y's knock - ing at your door. _____

170

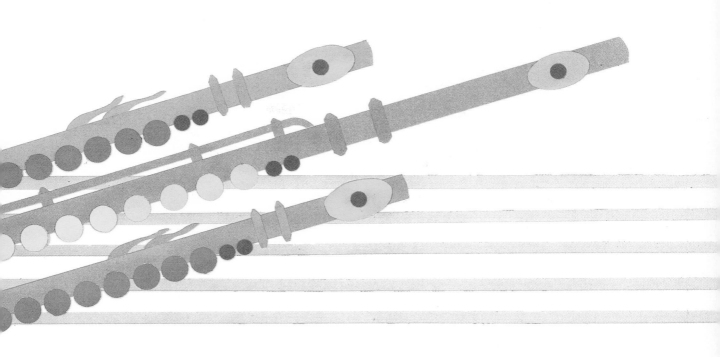

1. Knocks like the Lord._____
2. Can't you _____ hear Him?
3. An - swer the Lord._____

Knocks like the Lord: _____
Can't you _____ hear Him?
An - swer the Lord: _____

rit.

O _____ sin - ner, why don't you an - swer?

Some - bod - y's knock - ing at your door. _____

171

Many cultures around the world have their own kinds of flutes.

• Match each description of a flute with its picture on the right.

A. A **recorder** is a simple flute that is held downward. It has holes in front and is made of wood or plastic.

B. A **double recorder** has two mouthpieces and two sets of finger holes. The right hand plays simple melodies while the left hand plays an accompaniment. This recorder is from Yugoslavia.

C. A **nose flute** is played by placing the closed end of a bamboo tube under the nose. This flute is from the Philippines.

D. **Panpipes** are made of several lengths of connected hollow tubing. They are played by blowing across the tops of the tubes. They are found on every continent. This panpipe is from South America.

E. The **Native American carved flute** is held downward. The end is carved into the shape of an animal or figure.

F. The **oblique flute** is played at an angle, rather than straight down or to the side. These are from Niger, Africa.

G. Flutes have been made in many shapes and from many materials. This one is a walking stick. People can play music or walk with it.

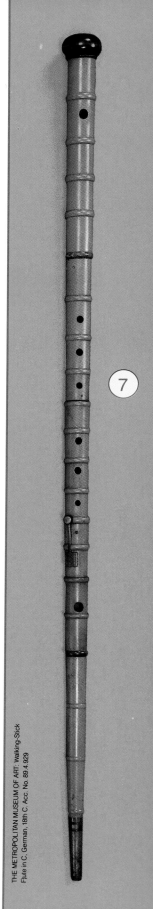

⑦

THE METROPOLITAN MUSEUM OF ART: Walking-Stick Flute in C, German, 18th C. Acc. No. 89.4.929

BERNICE PAUAHI BISHOP MUSEUM

5

2

4

3

1

6

THE MUSEUM OF THE AMERICAN INDIAN: Courting Flute,
Bird Head Carving, Witchita, Oklahoma

A HAUNTING STORY

● Notice which pitches are used in this song.

My Good Old Man

Traditional

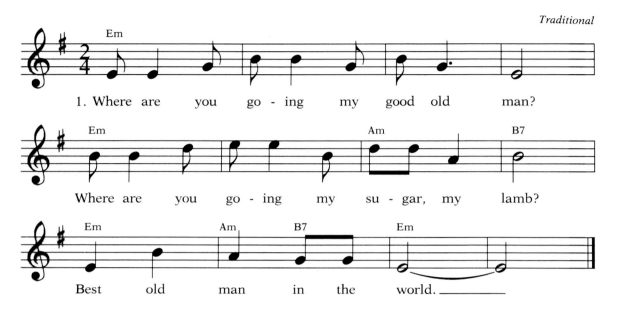

1. Where are you go - ing my good old man?

Where are you go - ing my su - gar, my lamb?

Best old man in the world. _____

(Spoken) I'm going to town.

2. What will you buy there my good old man?
   What will you buy there my sugar, my lamb?
   Best old man in the world.
   (Spoken) Bushel of eggs.

3. Bushel will kill you my good old man.
   Bushel will kill you my sugar, my lamb.
   Best old man in the world.
   (Spoken) Don't care if it does.

4. What for to die my good old man?
   What for to die my sugar, my lamb?
   Best old man in the world.
   (Spoken) So I can haunt you.

5. Why will you haunt me my good old man?
   Why will you haunt me my sugar my lamb?
   Best old man in the world.
   (Spoken) So I will always be near you.

The letter names of the lines and spaces of the staff are:

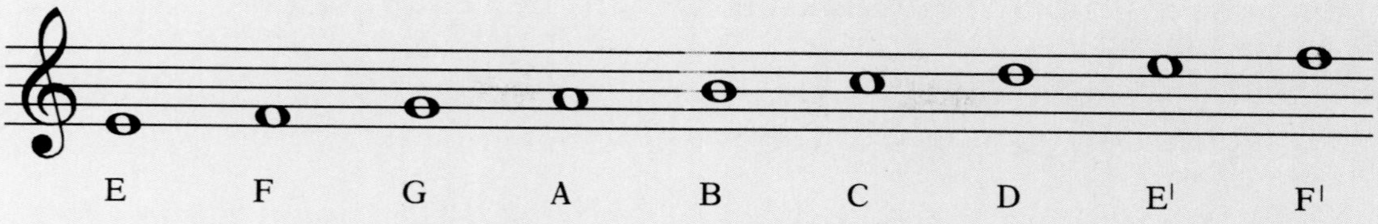

E   F   G   A   B   C   D   E'   F'

These are the six pitches in "My Good Old Man."

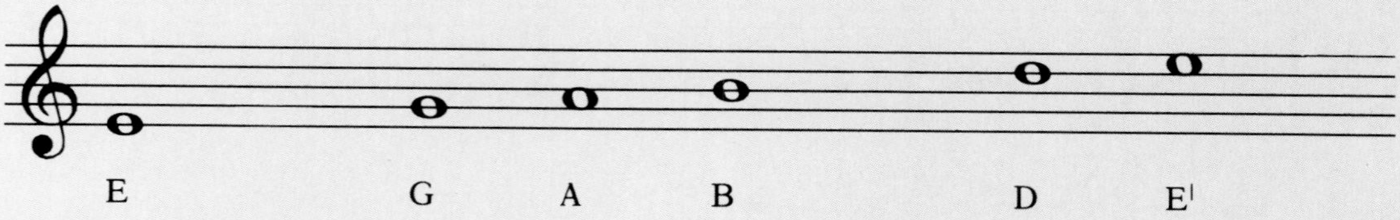

E   G   A   B   D   E'

- Play the song on bells.

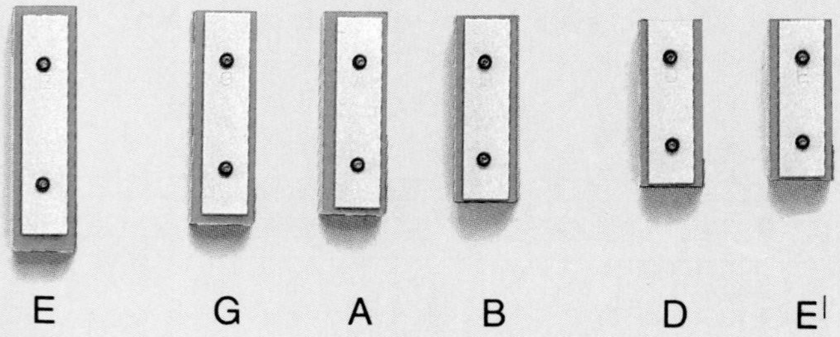

E   G   A   B   D   E'

MORE SYNCOPATED RHYTHM

● Find the syncopated rhythm patterns in the refrain of this song.

What words do you sing with these rhythms?

Open the Window, Noah

Refrain

Black American Spiritual

O - pen the win - dow, No - ah, O - pen the win - dow,

O - pen the win - dow, No - ah, O - pen the win - dow,

No - ah, O - pen the win - dow, No - ah,

No - ah, O - pen the win - dow, No - ah,

O - pen the win-dow, Let the dove come in. dove come in.

O - pen the win-dow, Let the dove come in. dove come in.

Verse

Solo D

1. The lit - tle dove flew in the win - dow and mourned, _
2. The lit - tle dove brought back the ol - ive ___ leaf, ___

All

D   A7   D

O - pen the win - dow, Let the dove come in.

O - pen the win - dow, Let the dove come in.

Solo A7   D

The lit - tle dove flew in the win - dow and mourned, _
The lit - tle dove brought back the ol - ive ___ leaf, ___

All

D   *D.C. (Last time al Fine)*
                                              A7   D

O - pen the win - dow, Let the dove come in.

O - pen the win - dow, Let the dove come in.

177

- Listen to Variations on the Theme "Pop! Goes the Weasel."
Follow the listening map.

Variations on the Theme "Pop! Goes the Weasel,"
by Lucien Caillet (loos-yen′ kä-yä′)

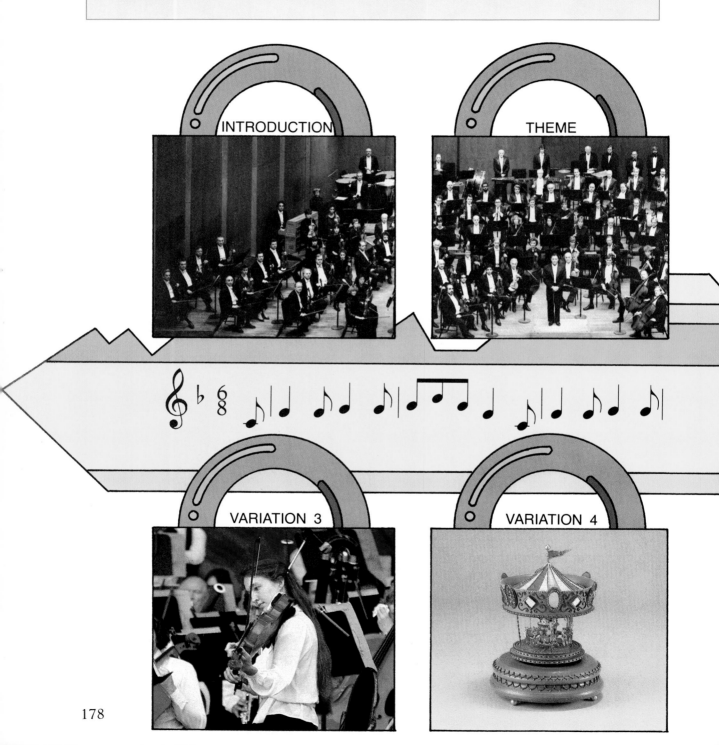

INTRODUCTION

THEME

VARIATION 3

VARIATION 4

178

Knowing the tune "Pop! Goes the Weasel" will be your key to unlocking the theme from its various "musical costumes."

VARIATION 1

Johann Sebastian Bach

VARIATION 2

Dancing the Minuet (detail)

POP

VARIATION 5

CODA

MAKE YOUR OWN VARIATIONS

● Create your own variation of a song.

Choose a song.
Decide which musical element you want to vary.
You can vary rhythm, melody, or tempo.
Decide how you will vary the musical
element. Practice the song. Then
practice the variation.

● Create your own
variation of this poem.

A kaleidoscope
Spinning, twirling forever
As the children play.
—*Anonymous*

● Read the poem. Now read it in a different way.

You have created a variation.

TAKE ANOTHER LOOK

Spring Variations

Scotland's Burning

Funga Alafia

Open the Window, Noah

● Ah, vous dirai-je, Maman

Artsa Alinu

● Russian Sailor's Dance

● Pop! Goes the Weasel

Do you remember?

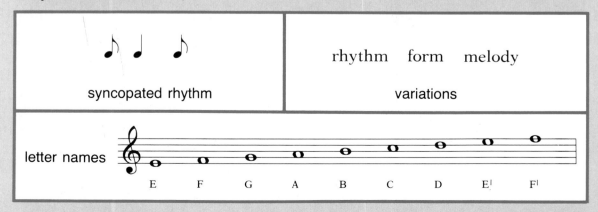

| syncopated rhythm | rhythm   form   melody |
| | variations |

letter names

E   F   G   A   B   C   D   Eʲ   Fʲ

182

JUST CHECKING

1. Tell three things a composer may change to make a variation.

2. Which have syncopated rhythms?

a.

b.

c.

d.

e.

f.

3. Look at this example.

a. What are the letter names of the pitches?
b. Does it have syncopated rhythm?
c. Name a song that begins this way.

FOCUS ON
Alice Parker

Alice Parker is a composer, conductor, and teacher. She has produced hundreds of arrangements of folk songs, hymns, and carols for the Robert Shaw Chorale. She has also written four operas, twelve cantatas, various songs, chamber music, a concerto for oboe and viola, and numerous settings of folk music.

Alice Parker was born in 1925 in Boston, Massachusetts. She started to play the piano when she was only five years old and to compose music when she was eight. She is a graduate of Smith College in Massachusetts and the Juilliard School of Music in New York. She gives lectures, leads workshops, and conducts her own works.

Alice Parker has always believed that music is a basic means of communication between people. She also believes that music can cheer you up when you feel blue and that the most important thing is to enjoy music.

Many in One

Words and music by Alice Parker

song,   And   love____ the soar-ing   mel-o-dy, the   mel-o-dy, the

mel-o-dy To   which   we   all   be-long.____

Man-y   are the   lan-guag-es   that

hu-man tongues em-ploy: ____   Man-y sounds and   i-di-oms that

speak   our grief and   joy: ____   But   one   is   the

or-i-gin and end-ing of the song,   And   love ____ the liv-ing

lan - guage,_ the lan - guage,_ the lan - guage _ To which we

all be - long; ___ And love ___ the cir - cling

rhy - thm,_ the soar - ing mel - o - dy,_ the liv - ing lan - guage _ To

which we all be - long. ___

© 1986, Augsburg Publishing House

UNIT 8

A MUSICAL JOURNEY THROUGH OUR COUNTRY

• What kinds of music
  might represent your
  hometown?

MUSICAL SIGNS

Musical signs are like road signs. They guide you through
the music.

- What different musical signs can you find?

- What does each tell you?

Here's to America

Words and music by Natalie Sleeth

Here's to   A - mer - i - ca!
{The land of the brave and the
{Of no - blest be - gin - nings is

free!   A   great   and might - y   na - tion   from
she!   Her   past   a wor - thy   bea - con   of

"sea to shin - ing   sea."}   Here's to   A - mer - i - ca!   {For -
faith and loy - al - ty. }   {And

ev - er may   she   be   a   coun - try strong   where
to   her his - to - ry,   To   all   the brave   who

all be - long in one dem - o - cra - cy.   ry.   Though
glad - ly gave their lives for _ vic - to -

woes may scar her spir - it, and foes as-sail her shore, may

she be blessed to meet the test of a - ges ev - er - more.

Here's to A - mer - i - ca! The cra - dle of lib - er - ty! A

blend of man - y peo - ple in one great u - ni - ty.

Here's to A - mer - i - ca! A light for all to see, I'll

sing her song my whole life long, for she is ___ home to

me, ___ A - mer - i - ca is home to me! ___

optional divisi

me, ___ for A - mer - i - ca is home to you and me. ___

191

• Tap the strong beat.

Down the River

River Chantey

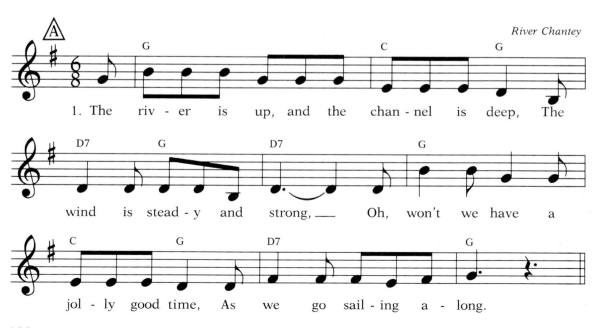

1. The riv-er is up, and the chan-nel is deep, The wind is stead-y and strong, ___ Oh, won't we have a jol-ly good time, As we go sail-ing a-long.

Refrain

Down the riv - er, Oh, down the riv - er, Oh,

Down the riv - er, Oh, down the riv - er, Oh,

down the riv - er we go. _____ Down the riv - er, Oh,

down the riv - er we go. _____ Down the riv - er, Oh,

down the riv - er, Oh, down the O - hi - o! _____

down the riv - er, Oh, down the O - hi - o! _____

2. The river is up, and the channel is deep,
   The wind is steady and strong,
   Oh, Dinah, put the hoecake on,
   As we go sailing along.
   Refrain

3. The river is up, and the channel is deep,
   The wind is steady and strong,
   The waves do splash from shore to shore,
   As we go sailing along.
   Refrain

- What does the meter signature in this song tell about how the beats are grouped?

Song of the Fishes

Sea Chantey

1. Come, all ye young sail-or-men, lis-ten to me, ___
2. Oh, first came the whale _ the big-gest of all, ___

I'll sing you a song of the fish of the sea.
He climbed up a-loft and let ev-ery sail fall.

Refrain

Then blow, ye winds west-er-ly, west-er-ly, blow, _

We're bound to the south-'ard, so stead-y she goes!

3. And next came the mack'rel with his striped back;
He hauled aft the sheets and boarded each tack.
Refrain

4. Then came the porpoise with his short snout;
He went to the wheel, calling "Ready about!"
Refrain

5. Then came the smelt, the smallest of all;
He jumped to the poop and sung out "Topsail, haul!"
Refrain

6. The herring came saying, "I'm king of the seas,
If you want any wind, why I'll blow you a breeze."
Refrain

7. Next came the cod with his chucklehead;
He went to the main-chains to heave at the lead.
Refrain

8. Last came the flounder as flat as the ground;
Says, "Listen here, chucklehead, mind how you sound!"
Refrain

This descant goes with the refrain.

● Sing or play it.

Descant for Voices, Bells, or Recorder (Refrain Only)

Then blow,   winds,   blow; ___   Blow,   winds, so   stead-y   she   goes!

- Tap the strong beat. How are the beats grouped?
- How _does_ this sign ⌢ affect your steady beat?

A Capital Ship

Words and music by Charles E. Carryl

1. A cap-i-tal ship for an o-cean trip Was the *Wal-lop-ing Win-dow Blind;*
2. The boat-swain's mate was ⏤ ver-y se-date Yet ⏤ fond ⏤ of a-muse-ment, too;

No gale that blew dis-mayed her crew, Or trou-bled the cap-tain's mind.
And he played hop-scotch with the star-board watch While the cap - tain tick-led the crew.

The man at the wheel was taught to feel Con-tempt for the wild-est blow, ⏤
And the gun-ner we ⏤ had was ap-par-ent-ly mad For he sat on the af-t er rail, ⏤

And it of-ten ap-peared, when the weath-er had cleared That he'd been in his bunk be-low.
And ⏤ fired ⏤ sa-lutes with the cap - tain's boots, In the teeth of the rag-ing gale.

Refrain

f G7   Ⓑ

C   F   C

Then blow, ye winds, heigh - ho! A - rov - ing I will go!

G7   C   F   C   F   G7

I'll stay no more on Eng-land's shore, So let the mu - sic play! _____

C   F   C

I'm off for the morn - ing train! I'll cross the rag - ing main!

G7   C   F   C   F   G7   C

I'm off to my love with a box - ing glove, Ten thou-sand miles a - way.

197

- Practice conducting these meters. Move your arm as if you are bouncing a tennis ball on the first beat of each measure.

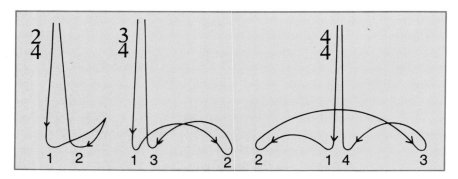

- Sing and conduct each song below. What is the meter for each song?

Join Hands in Brotherhood

Join hands in brotherhood from shore to shore,
Lift up your voice and sing,
Sing out "Let freedom ring,"
And to each nation bring peace evermore.

Yankee Doodle

Yankee Doodle went to town a-riding on a pony,
He stuck a feather in his cap and called it macaroni.
Yankee Doodle keep it up, Yankee Doodle dandy,
Mind the music and the step and with the girls be handy.

Are You Sleeping?

Are you sleeping, are you sleeping,
Brother John, Brother John?
Morning bells are ringing, morning bells are ringing,
Ding, ding, dong. Ding, ding, dong.

- Sing each song in a different meter.

198

FORM IN MUSIC

● How do you know that this song has two sections?

Buffalo Gals

American Folk Song

1. As I was walk-ing down the street, down the street, down the street, A

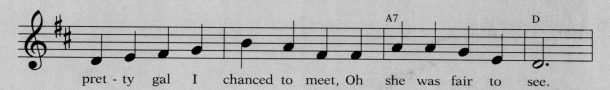

pret - ty gal I chanced to meet, Oh she was fair to see.

Refrain

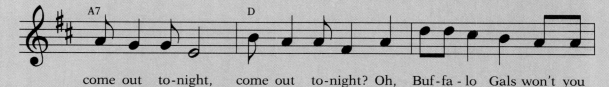

Oh, Buf - fa - lo Gals won't you come out to - night,

come out to-night, come out to-night? Oh, Buf-fa-lo Gals won't you

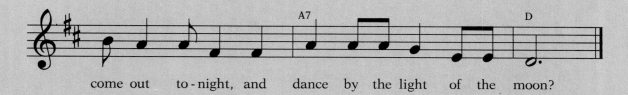

come out to - night, and dance by the light of the moon?

2. I asked her if she'd stop and talk, stop and talk, stop and talk,
   Her feet took up the whole sidewalk, and left no room for me.
   Refrain

3. I asked her if she'd be my wife, be my wife, be my wife,
   Then I'd be happy all my life, if she'd marry me.
   Refrain

- Find the phrases in this song.

- Which phrases have the same melody?

All Through the Night

Folk Song from the British Isles

1. Sleep, my child, and peace at-tend thee,
2. While the moon her watch is keep-ing,
} All through the night.

Guard-ian an-gels God will send thee,
While the wea-ry world is sleep-ing,
} All through the night.

Soft the drow-sy hours are creep-ing, Hill and vale in slum-ber steep-ing,
O'er thy spir-it gen-tly steal-ing, Vi-sion of de-light re-veal-ing,

I, my lov-ing vig-il keep-ing,
Breathes a pure and ho-ly feel-ing,
} All through the night.

- Sing this descant with all the phrases that are like the first phrase.

Sleep my child, ____ All through the night.

200

Béla Bartók used two different melodies as the themes of "Evening in the Village." A **theme** is a musical idea.

- Listen for the first theme. What instrument is featured?
- Raise your hand when the second theme begins. What instrument is featured?

 "Evening in the Village," from *Hungarian Sketches*, by Béla Bartók (bā′lə bär′täk)

BÉLA BARTÓK

Béla Bartók (1881–1945) was a Hungarian composer. He studied with famous composers, but soon found his own style. His music, often containing Hungarian folk melodies, is frequently performed throughout the world.

© G.D. Hackett, N.Y.

RHYTHMS THAT ARE ALIKE

● Find this rhythm combination  in this song.

The Rooster

Israeli Folk Song

In this song, are the rhythms of both lines the same? Are the
pitches of both lines the same?

Old Texas

Cowboy Song

1. I'm going to leave _____ old Tex-as now, _____
2. They've plowed and fenced _____ my cat-tle range, _____

They've got no use _____ for the long-horn cow. _____
And the peo-ple there _____ are all so strange. _____

3. I've roped and tied the dogies small,
   And listened for the coyote's call.

4. I'm gonna turn my back on the Texas sky,
   We'll ride away, old Paint and I.

5. Say "Adios" to the friends I know,
   I'll hit the trail for Mexico.

This accompaniment pattern makes a good introduction to
"Old Texas."

Leav-in' old Tex - as, leav-in' old Tex - as.

203

MELODIC SHAPES

- Move your hand up and down to follow these melodic shapes.

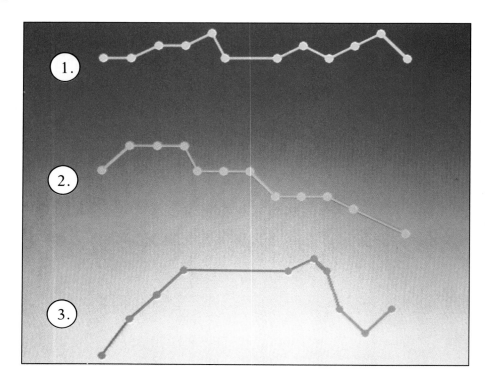

- Match the shapes to the music below.

THE WAY MELODY MOVES

Melody moves by steps, skips, and repeated tones.

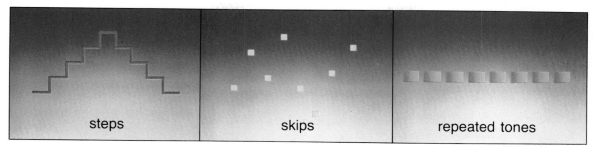

steps   skips   repeated tones

- Find steps, skips, and repeated tones in this song.

Ching-a-ring Chaw

American Minstrel Song

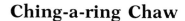
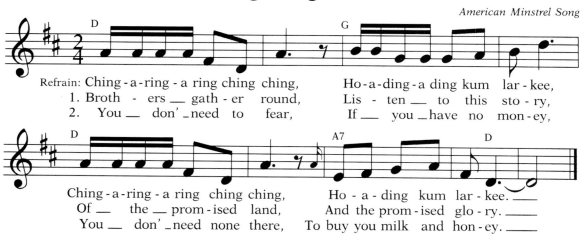

Refrain: Ching - a - ring - a ring ching ching,   Ho - a - ding - a ding kum lar - kee,
 1. Broth - ers __ gath - er   round,   Lis - ten __ to this sto - ry,
 2. You __ don' _ need to fear,   If __ you _ have no mon - ey,

Ching - a - ring - a ring ching ching,   Ho - a - ding kum lar - kee. ____
Of __ the __ prom - ised land,   And the prom - ised glo - ry. ____
You __ don' _ need none there,   To buy you milk and hon - ey. ____

3. There you'll ride in style,
   Coach with four white horses,
   There the evenin' meal,
   Has one, two, three, four courses.
   Refrain

4. Nights we all will dance,
   To the harp and fiddle,
   Waltz and jig and prance,
   "Cast off down the middle."

5. When the mornin' come,
   All in grand and splendor,
   Stand out in the sun,
   And hear the holy thunder.

6. Brothers hear me out,
   The promised land's a-comin',
   Dance and sing and shout,
   I hear them harps a-strummin'.
   Refrain

- Listen to a performance of this song by the Phoenix Boys Choir.

 "Ching-a-ring Chaw," from *Old American Songs,* by Aaron Copland (Version 1)

205

This song is from the American West. Dogies are motherless calves or calves that have strayed from the herd.

Git Along, Little Dogies

American Cowboy Song

1. As I was a-walk-ing one morn-ing for pleas-ure,
2. Now ear-ly in spring-time we round up the do-gies,
3. It's whoop-ing and yell-ing and driv-ing the do-gies,

I spied a cow-punch-er a-rid-ing a-long;
We mark them and brand them and bob off their tails;
Oh, how I wish you ___ would go right a-long;

His hat was thrown back and his spurs were a-jing-lin',
We drive up our hors-es and load the chuck wag-on,
It's whoop-ing and punch-ing, git on, lit-tle do-gies,

And as he ap-proached he was sing-ing this song.
Then throw ___ the do-gies out on-to the trail.
You know that Wy-o-ming will be your new home.

206

Refrain

Whoop-ee ti - yi - yo, git a - long, lit - tle do - gies,

It's your mis - for - tune and none of my own;

Whoop - ee ti - yi - yo, git a - long, lit - tle do - gies,

You know that Wy - o - ming will be your new home.

● Play this ostinato with "Git Along, Little Dogies."

● Play this descant with the refrain of "A Capital Ship" on page 196.

DOTTED RHYTHM

- Feel the difference between the rhythm of regular walking (♩ ♩ ♩ ♩) and the rhythm of walking on a sore foot (♩. ♪ ♩. ♪). Listen and move to "Sore Foot March." Change the way you walk as the rhythm changes.

"Sore Foot March"

- Clap the following rhythm. Plan your own way to show the notes that sound longer.

Here is the same pattern with one change.

- Tell what has been added. How will that change the sound?
- Clap this rhythm.

The pattern below may look different, but it sounds the same. A tie or a dot makes a note sound longer.

- Clap this rhythm. It sounds like the rhythm of the words "All through the night" on page 200.

A SHORT PIECE FOR WOODWIND QUINTET

Jacques Ibert composed this music for flute, oboe, clarinet, bassoon, and French horn. This group is called a **woodwind quintet** even though one of the instruments is not a woodwind.

- Name the instrument in a woodwind quintet that is not a woodwind.
- Follow the diagram below as you listen.

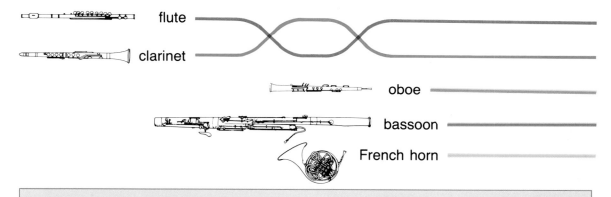

flute

clarinet

oboe

bassoon

French horn

 "Assez lent" from *Trois Pièces Brèves,* by Jacques Ibert (zhäk ē-bār')

JACQUES IBERT

Jacques Ibert (1890–1962) was a French composer and studied at the Paris Conservatoire. He wrote several important works while at the French Academy in Rome. After a busy composing career, he was appointed director of the Academy. Ibert wrote operas, ballets, and much choral, orchestral, and chamber music.

PLAYING WITH PITCHES

- Name these pitches. Play them on the bells or a keyboard.

The symbol ♯ in front of the first pitch on this staff is a **sharp.** It raises the sound a half step.

- Name these pitches.

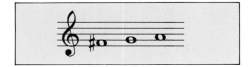

- Play this descant on bells with the refrain of "Ching-a-ring Chaw."

- Listen to the melody and descant of "I'm Gonna Sing." When F is to be F♯ throughout, a sharp is placed at the beginning of the music on the top line.

I'm Gonna Sing

Spiritual
Arranged by Carroll A. Rinehart

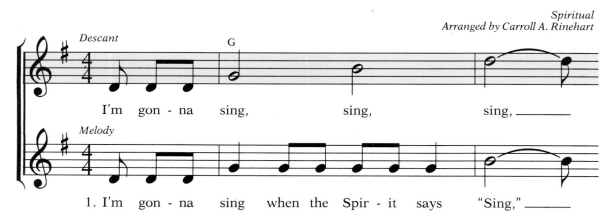

2. I'm gonna shout when the Spirit says "Shout,"
   I'm gonna shout when the Spirit says "Shout,"
   I'm gonna shout when the Spirit says "Shout,"
   And obey the Spirit of the Lord.

3. I'm gonna preach when the Spirit says "Preach,"
   I'm gonna preach when the Spirit says "Preach,"
   I'm gonna preach when the Spirit says "Preach,"
   And obey the Spirit of the Lord.

4. I'm gonna pray when the Spirit says "Pray,"
   I'm gonna pray when the Spirit says "Pray,"
   I'm gonna pray when the Spirit says "Pray,"
   And obey the Spirit of the Lord.

5. I'm gonna sing when the Spirit says "Sing,"
   I'm gonna sing when the Spirit says "Sing,"
   I'm gonna sing when the Spirit says "Sing,"
   And obey the Spirit of the Lord.

PLAYING F# ON THE RECORDER

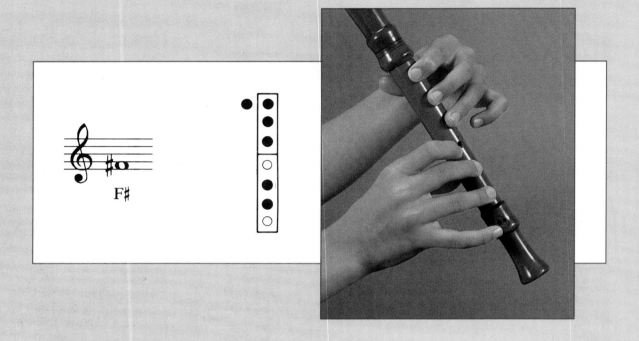

F#

Practice playing F# on the recorder by playing the descant for "Ching-a-ring Chaw" and this descant for "I'm Gonna Sing." Remember that the # at the beginning of the music means that every F will be an F#.

Use the pitches you can play on the recorder to create your own song.

SHARPEN YOUR LISTENING SKILLS

Here is a new version of "Ching-a-ring Chaw."

● Complete the statements below to describe what you hear.

 "Ching-a-ring Chaw," from *Old American Songs,* by Aaron Copland (Version 2)

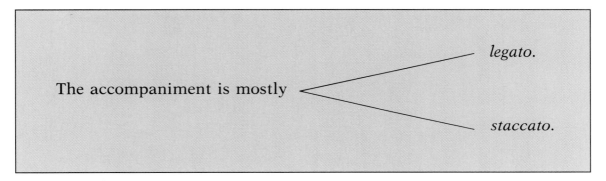

The accompaniment is mostly ⟨ legato. / staccato.

For each verse:

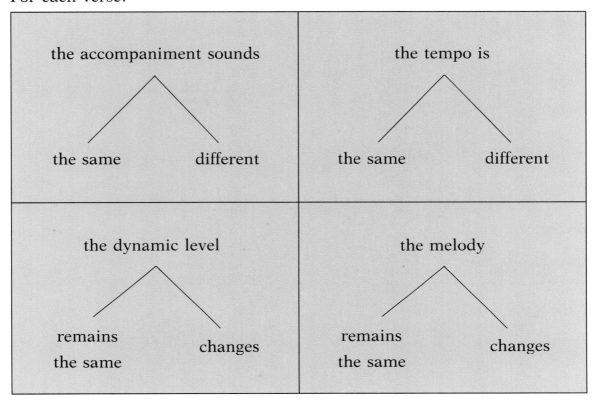

the accompaniment sounds — the same / different

the tempo is — the same / different

the dynamic level — remains the same / changes

the melody — remains the same / changes

TAKE ANOTHER LOOK

A Musical Journey

Here's to America

Ching-a-ring Chaw

Down the River

I'm Gonna Sing

Buffalo Gals

● Evening in the Village

Git Along,
Little Dogies

Song of the Fishes

A Capital Ship

All Through the Night

Do you remember?

notes

JUST CHECKING

1. Which pattern matches the word rhythm "blow, ye winds, heigh-ho" from "A Capital Ship" on page 196?

a.

b.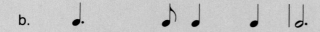

c.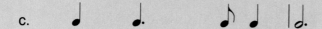

2. Name the pitches.

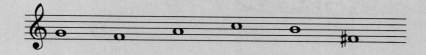

3. Name the song that begins this way:

Is the first pitch an F or an F♯?

Pets

A Musical Play by Wayne Chadwick

Pets

Words and music by Wayne Chadwick

1. Why don't you come and buy a pet to-day, ___

The ver-y fin-est you can get to-day. ___

Choose from the dogs and cats and birds and fish, ___

We're just the great-est pets you ev-er could wish! ___

Look a - round! __ There's Si - a - mese and e - ven

bas - set hound! __ Green tur - tles

and white mi - ces, And at such bar - gain pri - ces,

There's no - thing half as nice as pets!

2. Please step right in and buy a pet or two,
We're sure to have the perfect pet for you.
Our vast selection here is sure to please,
And you won't find much lower prices than these!
Come and see!
We're of the very highest quality!
Don't buy a home computer,
We're cheap and slightly cuter,
Come, everybody root for pets!

3. So please come on and lend a helping hand,
A bowl of water and a box of sand.
Our wants are simple and our needs are few,
A nice warm place to sleep and something to chew.
Here we wait,
So don't you wonder and procrastinate!
Just hurry, Jack, be nimble,
Beat drums and crash the cymbal,
Buy one of Mr. Kimball's pets!

217

Mr. Kimball's Pet Shop was a very special place. Here, pets who didn't quite fit in at other pet stores were taken in by Mr. Kimball. Here, he hoped that they would have another chance to find a home. But day after day went by and no one seemed to want to give a home to any of the animals. The pets became more and more unhappy. Of course, people who came into the shop looking for a pet did not want these grumpy, sad animals. Then along came Amy.

If I Only Had a Dog

Words and music by Wayne Chadwick

1. If I on-ly had a dog for a pet, for a pet,

If I on-ly had a dog for a pet it would be the great - est thing yet.

If I had a dog he'd sleep by my side,

Come and find me when I'd play a game and hide,

Run be-side me when I'd go for a ride on my bike.

That I'd like!

Ⓑ

But Mom says dogs are too big and ex-pen-sive,

Their man-ners are crude and their barks are in-ten-sive.

Poor lit-tle dog-gy, don't you get de-fen-sive,

Upper part last time only

But I guess that I can't have a dog.

2. If I only had a cat for a pet, for a pet,
   If I only had a cat for a pet, it would be the greatest thing yet.
   If I had a cat I'd rub her nice fur,
   Then I'd listen as she'd purr and she'd purr,
   And we'd never ever have to worry 'bout mice,
   That'd be nice.
   But Mom says cats make her eyes get all red,
   They bring bad luck, so her grandmother said,
   Sometimes I think that it's all in her head,
   But I guess that I can't have a cat.

3. If I only had a fish for a pet, for a pet,
   If I only had a fish for a pet, it would be the greatest thing yet.
   If I had a fish I'd watch him all day,
   Watch him swim in his wiggly way,
   And I'd watch while he played with his favorite toy,
   What a joy.
   But Mom says fish aren't good for a kid.
   I can do without just like her family did.
   It's not like I wanted an eighteen-foot squid,
   But I guess that I can't have a fish.

(Additional B section after verse 3)
I've asked and I've cried and I've hoped and I've begged,
For a bird or a fish or a creature four-legged,
But after twelve years, well, I've 'bout got it pegged,
And it's clear that I can't have a pet!

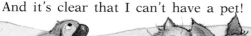

Unlike most people, Amy seemed to understand the pets. The pets were surprised and liked her right away. They told her about their problems. They told her about Mr. Kimball's kindness. They told her that more than anything else, they wanted to have a real home and . . . they wanted to be loved.

To Love and to Be Loved

Words and music by Wayne Chadwick

To love and to be loved,   To cher - ish and be   cher - ished,
To love and to be loved,   To share the joy of   liv - ing.

To share and share a - like,   To care for and to   be cared   for,
To give and to re - ceive,   And then to go on   giv - ing   more,

This is all we ask,   This is what we're search - ing   for.

220

When the win-ter comes, ___ and when comes the win-ter's blow-

- ing storm,

Noth-ing's quite so fair ___ as some-one who's al-ways there _

___ to keep you warm. ___

And when the way gets rough, And trou-bles o-ver-take us,

To know we'll make it through, 'Cause some-one's there to make us

strong, This is all we ask, This is all we ask,

This is what we're search-ing for. _____

Mr. Kimball heard all of the noise and came out of the back room where he had been doing his accounts. He looked very sad. Amy, who was very happy having met all the pets, asked what was wrong. Mr. Kimball told Amy that he was unable to pay the rent. He would soon lose the shop and the pets would have to be moved out in just a couple of days. The noise started all over again when the pets began trying to think of ways to help. But, none of their ideas seemed to be any good. Amy thought and thought and thought. Then she made a suggestion. She said that maybe the pets could do something to help Mr. Kimball if they all worked together.

Together

Words and music by Wayne Chadwick

To - geth - er, we can make ev - 'ry - thing work out right. ___
geth - er, we can make this old world look like new. ___

To - geth - er we can make the new day bright. ___
To - geth - er we can make our dreams come true. ___

Take my hand, come walk with me. ___
Lend a hand, come work with me. ___

We'll get there, just wait and see, ___

you and me. ___ To - ___

We can be ___ much more ___ to - geth - er than a - part, ___

Know - ing we ___ have friends ___ be - side ___ us from ___ the start, ___

For, to-geth-er,___ you see,_____

We can be what _ we want to be._____

Ⓐ

To-geth - er we can trav-el to worlds near and far._____

To - geth - er we can reach the high-est star._____

On our own we'll nev - er fly._____

All as one we'll soar up high,_____

Through the sky!_____ To - geth - er,_____

To - geth - er,_____ To - geth - er!_____

The pets decided that they would surprise Mr. Kimball and
build him a new pet shop. Amy promised not to tell
Mr. Kimball and spoil their surprise. However, she tried to
convince Mr. Kimball that the pet shop would somehow be
saved. Something was sure to happen.

Don't Ever Give Up Hope

Words and music by Wayne Chadwick

Don't ev-er give up hope, Mis-ter Kim-ball, ___ You must-n't give up
good, Mis-ter Kim-ball, ___ Done lots of no-ble

hope.
deeds.

I know that you have friends, Mis-ter Kim-ball,
Just think of them as seeds, Mis-ter Kim-ball,

friends who ___ real - ly care,
fal-len to the earth be - low,

And as long as you have
And in your time of

friends, Mis - ter Kim - ball, hope will still be there. _____
need, Mis - ter Kim - ball, some of them will

You've lived a life that's grow. _____

You can't al-ways tell who'll an - swer, or e - ven who will hear the

call. But re - mem - ber that some - times great things can be

done by ___ those who are small.

So don't you give up hope, Mis-ter Kim-ball, ___ You must-n't give up

now. When you have so man-y friends, Mis-ter Kim-ball,

friends who are good and true, Though you may not see

how, Mis-ter Kim-ball, friends will see you through.

Don't ev-er give up hope, You must-n't give up

hope.

(Spoken) Amy: Well, good night, Mr. Kimball.   Kimball: Good night, Amy.

227

The pets had only a few days to finish the new shop. After
the first day they were very tired. Some of them wanted to
give up. But Tabby the cat decided that what they needed
was a song.

Keep On

Words and music by Wayne Chadwick

1. When you're tired and your work seems nev-er-end - ing,

When suc-cess seems oh, so far a - way,

When all you see a - head is pain and trou - ble,

Then list - en, please list - en and do just-a what I say.

Refrain

Keep on,

Keep on try - ing, keep on do - ing your best.

228

Keep on, _____

Keep on try - ing, don't you stop __ to rest. __

Keep on, _____

Keep on try - ing, give it all that you've got. __

You've got to keep on keep - ing on. ____

You've got to keep on keep - ing on. ____

2. When the job seems more than you can handle,
   When every step seems to make you two steps behind,
   When all the weight of the world is on your shoulders,
   Then, brothers and sisters, just keep this song in mind.
   Refrain

3. So now we know when things are looking hopeless,
   When everything we do just turns out wrong.
   If we just work together we can find a better way,
   And while we are doing it we'll sing this happy song.
   Refrain (twice)

At last the pets finished the new shop. They were tired but happy. When the pets returned to the old shop that night they fell right asleep.

Early in the morning, Lucy the canary got up before any of the others were awake. She wanted to be the first to see their new shop. But she soon returned with terrible news. The building they had all worked so hard to finish had been knocked down to make way for a parking lot.

The pets were heartbroken at the news. But, they now were more determined than ever to save Mr. Kimball's Pet Shop. Before they could think of a new plan, Mr. Kimball arrived. He looked very tired and sad.

Right away, the pets forgot their own problems. They all gathered around Mr. Kimball to cheer him up.

Song: To Love and to Be Loved (reprise)

Just then, some people came into the shop. They saw that the pets were happy and excited. (The pets felt good because they had worked together to help Mr. Kimball.) Now the people thought the pets were wonderful and wanted to take them home.

Soon Mr. Kimball had enough money to pay the rent. Amy came in and everyone celebrated because Mr. Kimball's Pet Shop had been saved.

Song: Together (reprise)

SONGBOOK

- Name this tune.

Mystery Tune

Traditional

O, I'm Goin' to Sing

Southern Spiritual

O, I'm goin' to sing, goin' to sing, goin' to sing,

goin' to sing all a-long my way, O, I'm goin' to sing, goin' to sing,

goin' to sing, goin' to sing all a-long my way.

Coral

Folk Song

1. O sail-or come a-shore. What have you brought for me?
2. Did not take it from the ground, nor pick it from a tree;

Red cor - al, white cor - al, cor - al from the sea.
Lit-tle in - sects made it in the storm - y, storm - y sea.

Great Big House

American Play Party Song

1. Great big house in New Or-leans, For - ty stor - ies high, —

Ev - 'ry room that I been in, filled with chick - en pie.

2. Went down to the old mill stream to fetch a pail of water,
   Put one arm around my wife, the other round my daughter.

3. Fare thee well my darling girl, Fare thee well my daughter,
   Fare thee well my darling girl with the golden slippers on her.

Raccoon

Folk Song

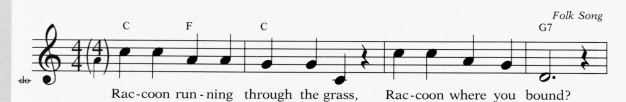

Rac-coon run - ning through the grass, Rac-coon where you bound?

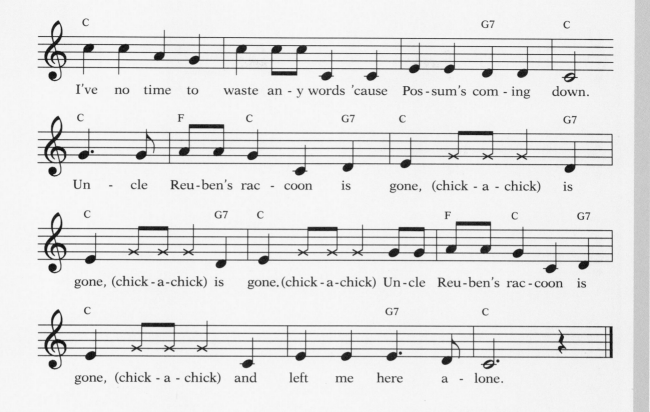

I've no time to waste an-y words 'cause Pos-sum's com-ing down.

Un - cle Reu-ben's rac - coon is gone, (chick - a - chick) is gone, (chick-a-chick) is gone. (chick-a-chick) Un-cle Reu-ben's rac-coon is gone, (chick - a - chick) and left me here a - lone.

Buckeye Jim

American Folk Song

1. Way down yon-der in a hol-low log, a blue jay danced with a green bull frog.____ Buck - eye Jim you can't go; Go
2. Way up yon-der a - bove the moon, a red bird lived in a sil - ver spoon.____

weave and spin, you can't go Buck-eye____ Jim.

Rattlesnake

Folk Song

Rat-tle-snake, O Rat-tle-snake, What makes your teeth so white?

I've been in the flat-lands all my life and I ain't done noth-in' but

bite, bite, Ain't done noth-in' but bite.

Ama Lama

Ohio Folk Song

A-ma la-ma coo-ma la-ma, coo-ma la-ma vee-stay.

Oh, no no no no no vee-stay,

Ee-nie mee-nie gyp-si-lee-nie, Oo ah oo ah mi-lee-nie,

Atch-y patch-y coo-mi-latch-y, I mean you!

The Old Sow

Arkansas Folk Song

1. What will we do with the old sow's hide?

Make as good cush-ion as ev-er did ride.

Coarse cush-ion, fine cush-ion, an-y such a thing,

The old sow died with the mea-sles in the spring.

2. What will we do with the old sow's tail?
Make as good whip as ever did sail.
Coarse whip, fine whip, any such a thing,
The old sow died with the measles in the spring.

3. What will we do with the old sow's meat?
Make as good bacon as ever was eat.
Coarse bacon, fine bacon, any such a thing,
The old sow died with the measles in the spring.

4. What will we do with the old sow's feet?
Make as good pickles as ever was eat.
Coarse pickles, fine pickles, any such a thing,
The old sow died with the measles in the spring.

5. What will we do with the old sow's head?
Make as good oven as ever baked bread.
Coarse oven, fine oven, any such a thing,
The old sow died with the measles in the spring.

Johnny Cuckoo

Black American Ring Play Song

1. Here comes one John-ny Cuck-oo, Cuck-oo, __ Cuck-oo.

Here comes one John-ny Cuck-oo on a cold and storm-y night.

2.,5. What did you come for, come for, come for,
What did you come for on a cold and stormy night?

3.,6. I come for me a soldier, a soldier, a soldier,
I come for me a soldier on a cold and stormy night.

4. Now here come two Johnny Cuckoos, Cuckoos, Cuckoos,
Here come two Johnny Cuckoos on a cold and stormy night.

Alabama Gal

Tennessee Play Party Song

1. You don't know how, how; You don't know how, how;
2. I'll show you how, how; I'll show you how, how;

You don't know how, how; Al - a - bam - a gal.
I'll show you how, how; Al - a - bam - a gal.

3. Ain't I rock candy?
   Ain't I rock candy?
   Ain't I rock candy?
   Alabama gal.

4. Come through in a hurry;
   Come through in a hurry;
   Come through in a hurry;
   Alabama gal.

America, the Beautiful

Words by Katharine Bates
Music by Samuel A. Ward
Arrangement by Mary Val Marsh

1. O beau-ti-ful for spa-cious skies, For am-ber waves of grain,
2. O beau-ti-ful for pa-triot dream that sees be-yond the years.

For pur-ple moun-tain maj-es-ties, A-bove the fruit-ed plain!
Thine al-a-bas-ter cit-ies gleam, Un-dimmed by hu-man tears!

A-mer-i-ca! A-mer-i-ca! God shed his grace on thee,

A-mer-i-ca! A-mer-i-ca!

And crown thy good with broth-er-hood, From sea to shin-ing sea.

And crown thy good From sea to shin-ing sea.

Arrangement Copyright ©1979 by Mary Val Marsh

Harvest

Georgian Folk Song

1. Time to gath - er har - vest. __

Oh, Em - ma, oh! _____

You turn a - round, dig a hole in the ground, __

Oh, Em - ma, oh!

2. Digging sweet potatoes,
   Oh, Emma, oh!
   You turn around, dig a hole in the ground,
   Oh, Emma, oh!

3. Digging rutabagas,
   Oh, Emma, oh!
   You turn around, dig a hole in the ground,
   Oh, Emma, oh!

4. Digging big fat parsnips,
   Oh, Emma, oh!
   You turn around, dig a hole in the ground,
   Oh, Emma, oh!

The First Noel

Traditional
Arranged by Carroll A. Rinehart

1. The first Noel, the an - gel did say,
2. They look - ed up and saw a star

Was to cer - tain poor shep - herds in fields as they lay;
Shin - ing in the east, be - yond them far,

In fields where they lay keep - ing their sheep,
And to the earth it gave great light,

On a cold win - ter's night that was so deep.
And so it con - tin - ued both day and night.

No - el, No - el, No - el, No - el,

No - el, No - el, No - el, No - el,

Born is the King of Is - ra - el.

Born is the King of Is - ra - el.

Joy to the World

Music Arranged from George F. Handel by Marilyn Rinehart
Words by Isaac Watts (from Psalm 98)

Descant

D   G   D   A7   D   G

1. Joy to the world! the Lord _ is __ come; Let earth _ re -
2. Joy to the world! the sav - ior _ reigns; Let men _ their _
3. He rules the world with truth _ and _ grace, And makes _ the _

Melody

1. Joy to the world! the Lord   is   come; Let earth   re -
2. Joy to the world! the Sav - ior   reigns; Let men   their
3. He rules the world with truth   and   grace, And makes   the

A7   D   G   D   G

ceive _ her _ King; Let ev - 'ry __ heart __ pre - pare Him _
songs _ em - ploy; While fields   and _ floods, _ rocks, hills   and _
na - tions _ prove The glo - ries _ of ____ his righ - teous -

ceive   her King; Let ev - 'ry __ heart __ pre - pare Him _
songs   em - ploy; While fields _ and _ floods, _ rocks, hills, _ and _
na - tions prove The glo - ries _ of ____ his righ - teous -

Arrangement Copyright ©1979 by Marilyn Rinehart

room, ___ / plains ___ / ness, ___   Heav'n and na-ture sing! / Sing the sound-ing joy! / Won-ders of His love!

room, ___ And heav'n and na-ture _ sing,   And _ heav'n and na-ture / plains ___ Re - peat the sound-ing_ joy,   Re - peat the sound-ing / ness, ___ And won-ders of His _ love,   And _ won-ders of His

Heav'n and na - ture sing!   And heav'n _ and na - ture sing. / Sing the sound - ing joy,   Re - peat ___ the sound - ing joy. / Won - ders of His love!   And won - ders of ___ His love.

sing,   And _ heav'n, _ and heav'n _ and na - ture sing. / joy,   Re - peat, _ re - peat ___ the sound - ing joy. / love,   And _ won - ders, won - ders of His love.

Pray God Bless

Traditional Canon

Pray God bless all friends here. A mer - ry, mer - ry Christ - mas and a hap - py New Year.

A la claire fontaine

French-Canadian Folk Song
English words adapted by M.S.

A la clai - re fon - tai - ne M'en al - lant pro - me - ner,
I walked be - side the foun - tain Once on a sum - mer day,

J'ai trou - vé l'eau si bel - le Que je m'y suis bai - gné.
Cool wa - ter was in - vit - ing So I did not de - lay.

Lui ya long - temps que je t'ai - me,
There at the fount I re - mem - ber

Ja - mais je ne t'ou - blie - rai.
How I miss you more each day.

Aardvarks on the Ark

Words and music by Mary Val Marsh
Based on a spiritual

Who built the ark! No - ah, No - ah;

Who built the ark? Broth - er No - ah built the ark. Say!

No - ah built the ark. He had

an - i - mals of ev - 'ry size and shape! He had

an - i - mals of ev - 'ry kind that you can name. He had you can name.

Bongos (same tempo as above)
R.H.
L.H.

*Spoken, in rhythm
with expressive inflection*

Group I

1. There were
2. There were

243

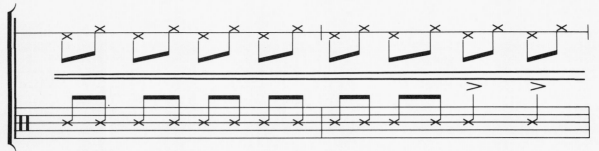

crick - ets small, gi - raffes so tall, and an - te - lopes and liz - ards!
big black bears and kan - ga - roos, and el - e - phants and AARD - VARKS!

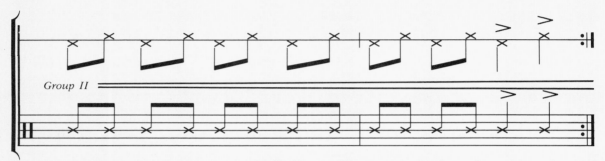

Group II

Ze - bras striped and pea - cocks bright, and an - i - mals with giz - zards!
Small rac - coons and por - cu - pines, and cats and dogs, but NO SHARKS!

Bongos   *(3 times)*

23

Then it rained and rained and rained and rained and

Oh!   my,   It   rained and rained and rained and then it

1.   2.

rained   some   more.   Yes,   it   rained   some   more.

Woodblock

Bongos

(Start softly and increase volume gradually)
(All)

Now once a-board that gi-ant boat they

W.B.

B.

all be-gan to talk; The sound a-round was so in-tense it

W.B.

34

B.

May be spoken by small groups or individuals.
Add appropriate vocal and/or instrumental
sound effects (SE) cumulatively.

made the great ark rock. Ducks quacked! (SE) Wolves howled! (SE)

W.B.

B.

Snakes hissed! (SE) Ti - gers growled! (SE)

Mon - keys chat - tered! (SE)   Don - keys brayed! (SE)

Hors - es   clat - tered! (SE)   Man - tis - es prayed.

All instruments silent
No ritard

pp

42

All sound effects above enter ad lib to achieve crescendo as indicated.

mf ————————————————————— *ff*

(Sounds fade quickly)

Then it

(Descant)

(Melody)
Say,

Annabelle

Traditional Camp Song

An - na - belle, where are you go - ing?

Up - stairs to take a bath.

Your legs are like two tooth - picks.

Your neck like a gir - affe!

An - na - belle, pull out the stop - per.

An - na - belle, look down the drain.

Oh, my good - ness, oh, my soul, there goes An - na - belle down that hole!

An - na - belle! An - na - belle! Glug!

248

Doktor Eisenbart

Pennsylvania Dutch Song

1. Oh, I am Dok-tor Ei-sen-bart, Twil-li, wil-li, witt boom boom!
2. Oh, I am Doc-tor I-ron-beard, Twil-li, wil-li, witt boom boom!

I cure your ill-ness with my art, Twil-li, wil-li, witt boom boom!
My pa-tients think I'm ver-y weird, Twil-li, wil-li, witt boom boom!

Now I can help the mute to walk, Twil-li, wil-li, witt boom boom boom boom!
I've pep-per just to make them sneeze, Twil-li, wil-li, witt boom boom boom boom!

The lame to see, the blind to talk, Twil-li, wil-li, witt boom boom!
And pol-len that will make them wheeze, Twil-li, wil-li, witt boom boom!

Refrain

Sing tor-i-ay, sing tor-i-ay! Twil-li, wil-li, witt boom boom boom boom!

Sing tor-i-ay, sing tor-i-ay! Twil-li, wil-li, witt boom boom!

249

Dumplin's

West Indies Calypso Song

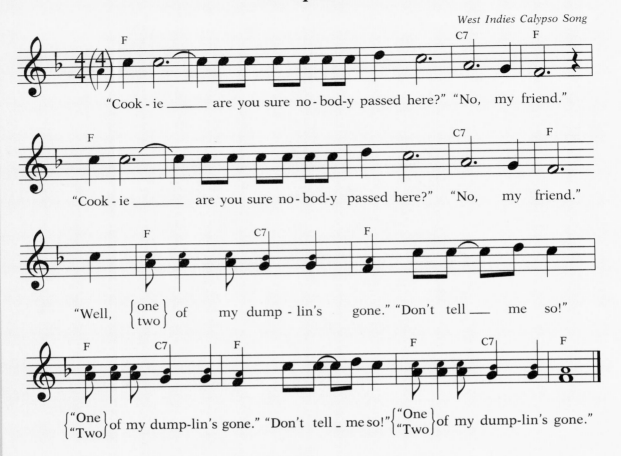

"Cook - ie _____ are you sure no - bod-y passed here?" "No, my friend."

"Cook - ie _____ are you sure no - bod-y passed here?" "No, my friend."

"Well, { one / two } of my dump - lin's gone." "Don't tell __ me so!"

{ "One / "Two } of my dump-lin's gone." "Don't tell _ me so!" { "One / "Two } of my dump-lin's gone."

DUMPLIN'S
New words and new music adaptation by Massie Patterson and Sammy Heyward. TRO—© 1963 Ludlow Music, Inc., New York, N.Y. Used by Permission.

The Goat

French Folk Song
English Text by Alan Mills

1. Oh, once there was a goat, a ver-y cle-ver goat;
Il é - tait un - e chèvre de fort tem - pé - ra - ment,

Spoke French and Ger-man flu - ent - ly, as you will note!
Qui re - ve - nait d'Es-pagne et par - lait al - le - mand!

Refrain

Oh! Tra - la - la - la - la, Tra - la - la - la - la,

Spoke French and Ger-man flu - ent - ly, as you will note!
Qui re - ve - nait d'Es-pagne et par - lait al - le - mand!

2. This goat, he crossed the sea
from Spain to Germany,
And ended up upon a farm in
Normandy.
Oh, Tra-la-la-la-la,
Tra-la-la-la-la-la,
And ended up upon a farm in
Normandy.

3. And once upon that farm,
he thought—without alarm—
To steal a cabbage there could
surely do no harm.
Refrain

4. But tho' no harm was meant,
the farmer did resent,
And had the goat arrested and to
trial sent.
Refrain

5. You may think this absurd,
but when the case was heard,
That clever goat, the law recited
word by word.
Refrain

6. But ere the verdict came,
he knew he was to blame,
So off he ran while all the judges
cried out "Shame."
Refrain

251

Giddap, Old Dobbin

Dutch Tune

Melody 1

1. Gid-dap, old Dob-bin, we're go-in' to town, Let's get those wheels a-
2. Gid-dap, old Dob-bin, the shop-pin' is done, The bug-gy is load-ed; gid-

turn-in' a - round, Let's get those wheels a - turn-in' a - round,
dap, la-zy one, Let's get those wheels a - turn-in' a - round,

There's miles to go be - fore sun - down.
We got to get home be - fore sun - down.

Melody 2

I like to drive the horse and bug-gy, When I go

trav-'ling to the town; I like to hear old Dob-bin's

clip, clop, I like to feel the wheels go 'round.

Melody 3

1. Dob-bin, Dob-bin on your way, We've been to-geth-er for
2. Dob-bin, Dob-bin don't you stop, Just let your feet go

man - y a day, So let your tail go swish as the
clip - pe - ty clop And let your tail go swish as the

wheels go 'round, Gid - dy - ap! We're home - ward bound.
wheels go 'round, Gid - dy - ap! We're home - ward bound.

Head and Shoulder, Baby

Words and music by Bessie Jones

1. Head   and shoul - der, ba - by,
2. Knee   and an - kle, ba - by,   } one,   two,   three.
3. Milk   the cow, __ ba - by,
4. Throw the ball, __ ba - by,

Head   and shoul - der, ba - by,
Knee   and an - kle, ba - by,   } one,   two,   three.
Milk   the cow, __ ba - by,
Throw the ball, __ ba - by,

Head   and shoul - der, head   and shoul - der, head   and shoul - der, ba - by,
Knee   and an - kle, knee   and an - kle, knee   and an - kle, ba - by,
Milk   the cow, __ milk   the cow, __ milk   the cow, __ ba - by,
Throw the ball, __ throw the ball, __ throw the ball, __ ba - by,

one,   two,   three.

"Head and Shoulder, Baby," words and music by Bessie Jones. Collected and edited with new material by Alan Lomax. TRO—© Copyright 1972 Ludlow Music, Inc., New York, N.Y. Used by Permission.

If I Had a Hammer

Words and music by
Lee Hays and Pete Seeger

1. If I had a ham-mer, — I'd ham-mer in the
2. If I had a bell, _____ I'd ring it in the
3. If I had a song, _____ I'd sing it in the
4. Well, I've got a ham-mer, — And I've __ got a

morn - ing, __ I'd ham-mer in the eve - ning, __
morn - ing, __ I'd ring it in the eve - ning, __
morn - ing, __ I'd sing it in the eve - ning, __
bell, _____ And I've __ got a song, _____

all o - ver this land; I'd ham-mer out
all o - ver this land; I'd ring __ out
all o - ver this land; I'd sing __ out
all o - ver this land; It's the ham-mer of

dan - ger, — I'd ham-mer out a warn - ing, __
dan - ger, — I'd ring __ out a warn - ing, __
dan - ger, — I'd sing __ out a warn - ing, __
jus - tice, — It's the bell __ of __ free - dom, —

I'd ham-mer out
I'd ring __ out
I'd sing __ out   love be-tween all of my broth-ers,
It's the song a-bout

All _____ o - ver this land. _____

IF I HAD A HAMMER
(The Hammer Song)
Words and music by Lee Hays and Pete Seeger. TRO—© 1958 (renewed 1986) and 1962 Ludlow Music, Inc., New
York, N.Y. Used by Permission.

I'se the B'y

Newfoundland Folk Song

1. I'se the b'y that builds the boat, I'se the b'y that sails her.
2. I took Li - za to the dance; Faith, but she could trav - el.
3. Su - san White is out of sight, Hid - ing like Jack Hor - ner.

I'se the b'y that catch - es the fish And brings them home to Li - za.
Ev - 'ry step that Li - za took ___ Cov - ered an a-cre of grav - el.
Choose a lad and take ___ him back, ___ Kiss him in the cor - ner.

Refrain

Swing your part - ner, Sal - ly Tib - ble, Swing your part - ner, Sal - ly Brown.

Swing your part - ner, ev - 'ry-one, All a - round ___ the cir - cle.

We Shall Overcome

American Freedom Song

1. We shall o - ver - come, _____ We shall o - ver - come, _____
2. We'll walk hand in hand, _____ We'll walk hand in hand, _____

We shall o - ver - come some day; _____ Oh, _____
We'll walk hand in hand some day; _____ Oh, _____

deep in my heart I do be - lieve,
deep in my heart I do be - lieve,

We shall o - ver - come some day. _____
We'll walk hand in hand some day. _____

3. We are not afraid,
   We are not afraid,
   We are not afraid today.
   Oh, deep in my heart I do believe,
   We are not afraid today.

4. We shall brothers be,
   We shall brothers be,
   We shall brothers be some day.
   Oh, deep in my heart I do believe,
   We shall brothers be some day.

5. Truth shall make us free,
   Truth shall make us free,
   Truth shall make us free some day.
   Oh, deep in my heart I do believe,
   Truth shall make us free some day.

Lots o' Fish in Bonavist' Harbor

Newfoundland Folk Song
Collected by Kenneth Peacock

1. There's lots o' fish in Bon - a - vist' Har - bor,
2. Oh, Sal - ly went to church ev - 'ry Sun - day,

Lots o' fish right in a - round here. Boys and girls are
Not for to sing nor for to hear. But to see the

fish - in' to - geth - er, For - ty - five from Car - bon - ear.
fel - ler from For - tune What was down here fish - in' last year.

Refrain

Oh, catch - a - hold this one, catch - a - hold that one,

Swing a - round this one, swing a - round she;

Dance a - round this one, dance a - round that one,

Did - dle dum dee dum, did - dle dum dee.

Move into Music

1. Come on and move into music, move into music,
     Move, move, move, move,
   Move into music—now!

2. Come on and clap to the music, clap to the music,
     Clap, clap, clap, clap,
   Clap to the music—now!

3. Come on and snap to the music, snap to the music,
     Snap, snap, snap, snap,
   Snap to the music—now!

4. Now move your knees to the music,
     move your knees to the music,
     Move, move, move, move,
   Move your knees to the music—now!

   Come on and move, move, move, move,
   Move, move, move, move,
   Move into music, move into music,
   Move into music, NOW!

5. Now let's walk to the music, walk to the music,
     Walk, walk, walk, walk,
   Walk to the music—Now!

6. Now let's hop to the music, hop to the music,
     Hop, hop, hop, hop,
   Hop to the music—Now!

7. So let's move—into music, move—into music,
     Move, move, move, move,
   Move into music now, move into music now,
   Come on and move into music—NOW!

Words and music by Barbara Staton

258

Niño Querido

Spanish Folk Song and Canon

Ni - ño que - ri - do, duér - me - te ya,
My lit - tle ba - by, sleep - ing there,

Que mien - tras tan - to te can - ta ma - má.
While Moth - er sings to her ba - by fair.

Ni - ño que - ri - do, duér - me - te ya.
My lit - tle ba - by, sleep - ing there.

Papageno's Song

Music by Wolfgang A. Mozart
Words by Mary Val Marsh

1. I __ am a sim - ple, _ qui-et man, I __ play up-on my pipes of Pan.
2. I __ am a sim - ple, _ qui-et man, I __ play up-on my pipes of Pan.

Of catch-ing _ birds _ I __ make a game, And Pa - pa - ge - no is my name.
I like _ to __ catch _ my _ feath-ered friends, But that's not where my sto-ry ends;

I __ whis - tle and _ I __ spread my net, And then some pret - ty _ birds I get,
I __ wish that when _ I __ spread my net, A hun-dred pret - ty _ girls I'd get,

I __ roam the woods _ so _ ver - y free, A __ hap-py man _ I'll _ al - ways _ be.
I'd _ choose the fair - est _ one for me, A __ hap-py man _ I'd _ sure-ly _ be.

Rock Island Line

American Folk Song

Oh, the Rock Is - land Line is a might-y fine road, _

Oh, the Rock Is - land Line is the road _ to ride. _

Oh, the Rock Is - land Line is a might-y fine road, _

If you want to ride, you got to ride it like you find it,

Get your tick - et at the sta - tion on the Rock Is - land Line.

1. A B C dou-ble X Y Z, Cat's in the cup - board
2. No - bod-y cares for the rail - road man, You're gon - na miss _

but she can't see me. _
me _

when I'm gone. _

Roll On, Columbia

Music based on "Goodnight Irene"
by Huddie Ledbetter and John Lomax
Words by Woody Guthrie

1. Green Doug-las fir where the wa-ters cut through,
2. Oth-er big riv-ers add power to you,

Down her wild moun-tains and can-yons she flew.
Yak-i-ma, Snake, and the Klick-i-tat, too.

Ca-na-di-an North-west to the o-cean so blue,
Sand-y, Wil-lam-ette, and the Hood Riv-er, too,

Roll on, Co-lum-bia, roll on.

Refrain

Descant

Melody

Roll on, Co-lum-bia, roll on. Roll on, Co-

lum-bia, roll on. Your pow-er is turn-ing our

dark-ness to dawn, Roll on, Co-lum-bia, roll on.

262 ROLL ON, COLUMBIA
Words by Woody Guthrie. Music based on "GOODNIGHT IRENE" by Huddie Ledbetter & John A. Lomax.
TRO—© Copyright 1936 (renewed 1964), 1950 (renewed 1978), 1957 (renewed 1985) and 1963 Ludlow Music,
Inc., New York, N.Y. Used by Permission.

Sit on the Green Grass

Words and music by Patti Schliestett-Wiggins

1. Sit on the green grass, sing me a song;
2. Sit on the green grass, sing me a song;
3. Now all to-geth-er sing-ing our song;

Hear all the co-co-nuts play-ing a-long.
Hear all the lit-tle sticks play-ing a-long.
Hear all the in-stru-ments play-ing a-long.

Refrain

La la la la la, la la la la;

Sing a ca-lyp-so song.

263

Sweetly Sings the Donkey

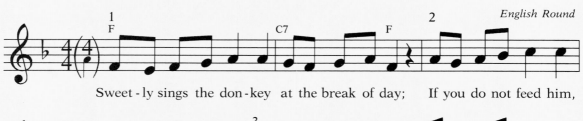

English Round

Sweet-ly sings the don-key at the break of day;   If you do not feed him,

this is what he'll say,   "Hee-haw! Hee-haw! Hee-haw, hee-haw, hee-haw!"

Swinging Along

Traditional

Descant

Swing-ing a-long   the   o - pen road

Melody

Swing-ing a - long _____ the o - pen road   un-der a

Swing-ing   a-long   un-der a   sky   that's   clear.

sky   that's   clear.   Swing-ing a -

Swing-ing a-long the o-pen road All in the fall, in the

long _____ the o-pen road In the fall of the

fall of the year. Swing-ing a-long, swing-ing a-long, swing-ing a-

year. Swing-ing a-long, swing-ing a-long, swing-ing a-

long the o-pen road, __ All in the fall of the year.

long the o-pen road All in the fall of the year.

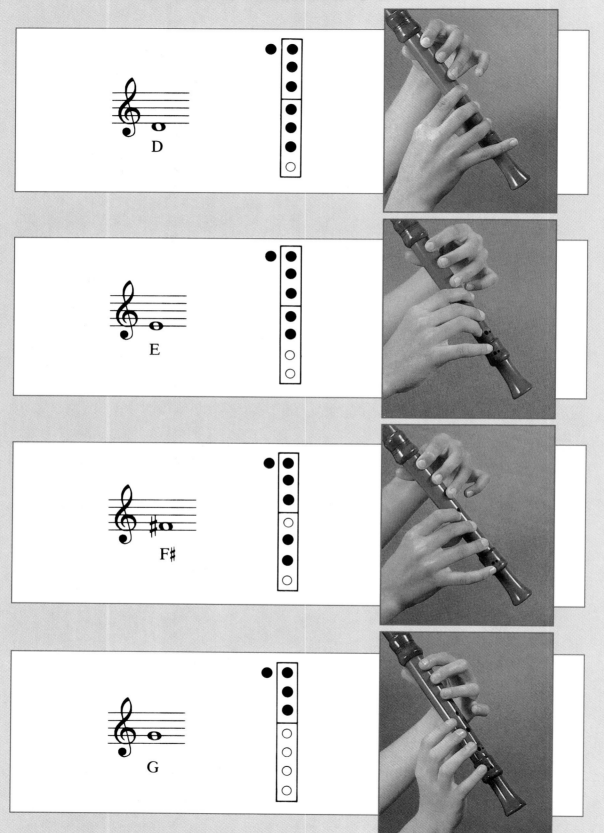

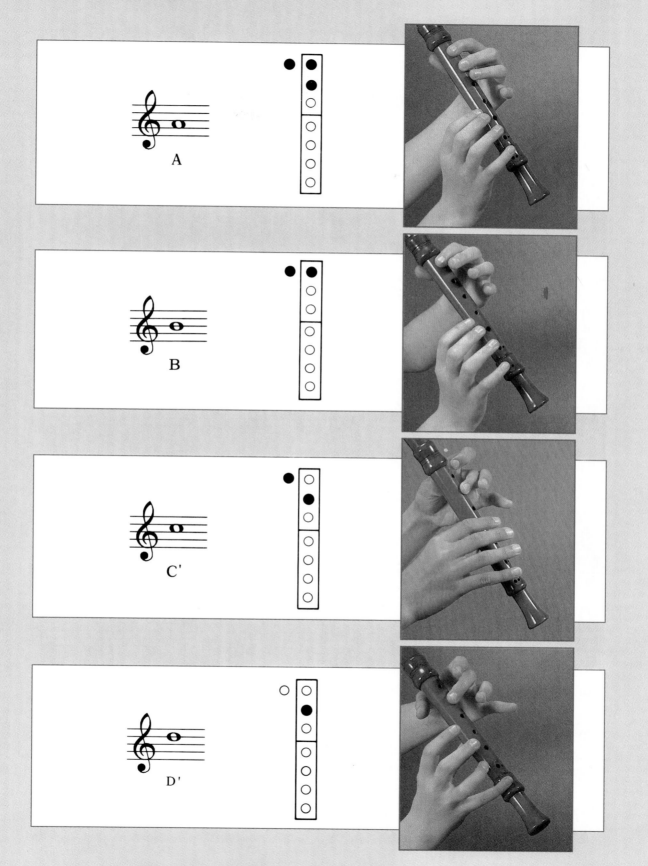

267

Recorder Boogie

Created by Dorothy Gail Elliott

- Look for the sign ♮ in "High 'D' Boogie." It is called a **natural.** It means that the C is not played as C♯ but as a C.
- Learn to play these two songs on the recorder. They may be played together.
- Play them together with a partner.

High "D" Boogie

Music by Dorothy Gail Elliott

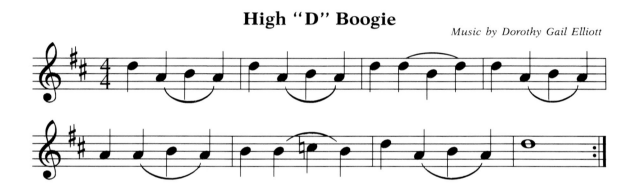

Low "D" Boogie

Music by Dorothy Gail Elliott

GLOSSARY OF TERMS

accelerando to gradually get faster, 71

accompaniment a musical background for the melody, 101

allegro fast, lively, 142

beat the basic unit of time in music, 2

chord a combination of three or more pitches sounded together, 139

chord root the pitch on which the chord is built, and which gives the chord its name, 139

coda an ending section to a piece of music, 167

composer a person who writes music, 184

crescendo (<) to get louder gradually, 84

descant a simple melody that is higher than the main melody, 131

dynamics softness and loudness in music, 43

eighth note (♪), 16

fermata (⌒) a symbol over a note that means the note should be held longer than its written value, 104

flat (♭) a symbol that means a tone should be lowered by a half step, 88

form the order of sections in music, 22

forte (*f*) loud, 84

fortissimo (*ff*) very loud, 48

half note (♩), 3

half step the distance between a pitch and the next closest pitch on a keyboard, 31

harmony two or more tones sounded at the same time, 110

improvise to make up music on the spot within given guidelines, 144

introduction music that comes before a song or other musical composition, 60

lento slow, 142

major a scale of tones arranged in terms of whole and half steps: W W H W W W H, 88

measure a set of notes and rests between two bar lines, 32

melody the tune; a series of pitches moving upward, downward, or staying the same, 10

meter beats grouped by sets in a piece of music, 32

meter signature the symbol at the beginning of each song that tells how many beats are in each measure and the kind of note that gets one beat, 32

mezzo forte (*mf*) medium loud, 136

mezzo piano (*mp*) medium soft, 136

minor a scale of tones arranged in terms of whole steps and half steps: W H W W H W W, 88

minuet a stately French court dance, 37

269

musical conversation instruments or singers taking turns playing or singing, **12**

octave the distance between two pitches having the same name and located twelve half steps apart, **54**

ostinato a rhythm or melody pattern that repeats, **102**

overture an orchestral piece written as an introduction to a larger musical work, for example, an opera, **92**

pentatonic scale a five-tone scale, **120**

phrase a short section of music that is one musical thought, **8**

pianissimo (pp) very soft, **48**

piano (p) soft, **84**

pitch the highness or lowness of a tone, **30**

presto very fast, **142**

quarter note (♩), 2

quarter rest (𝄽), 109

refrain a section of a song that is repeated after each verse; sometimes called a chorus, **195**

rhythm pattern an organized group of long and short sounds, **36**

ritard to get slower gradually, **72**

round a melody which can be repeated over and over, sung by two or more groups starting at different times, **83**

scale a series of pitches arranged in upward or downward order, **120**

sharp (♯) a symbol indicating that a sound is to be raised a half step, **210**

staff the five lines and four spaces on which music is written, **15**

strong beat the first beat after each bar line, **32**

syncopated rhythm rhythm that puts accents on beats that are normally not accented, **166**

tempo the speed of the beat, **70**

texture the thickness or thinness of sound that results when sounds are played or sung together, **83**

theme a musical idea, **201**

tie (⌣) a curved line that connects two notes of the same pitch and means that the sound should be held for the length of both notes, **141**

tone color the sound that is special to each instrument or voice, **42**

variation part of a musical form which begins with a theme, followed by a number of versions of it, each of these being a variation; the rhythm, melody, tone color, or other musical elements may be varied, **159**

whole note (o), 6

whole step the distance between two pitches having two half steps between them, **31**

woodwinds one of the four instrument families in the orchestra; they are played by blowing air through them, **4**

CLASSIFIED INDEX

LISTENING SELECTIONS

ALPHABETICAL SONG INDEX

(Photo credits continued from page v)

Depth of Case: 273 mm.; Edwin M. Ripin Collection, Friends of the Collection Fund, 75TR. NASA: 22, 23. NEW YORK PHILHARMONIC with ZUBIN MEHTA, musical director: © Harry Grossinsky, 178TL,TR, 179BR. ODYSSEY PRODUCTIONS: © Robert Frerck, 189TR,BR. OPERA NEWS: Alban Berg, b. 1885, Austrian, 9. © ALICE PARKER: 184. PHOTO RESEARCHERS, INC.: © William Bacon III, 56; © Van Bucher, 179TL. THE PICTURE CUBE: © Rick Friedman, 166–7TC. RAINBOW: © Hank Morgan, 126–7B; © Dan McCoy, 157L. RETNA, LTD., © Gary Gerschoff, 127TC. COURTESY ESTATE OF NORMAN ROCKWELL: 25, 73. SALSBERY ASSOCIATES, INC.: 65. STOCK BOSTON: © Elizabeth Crews, 36; © Milton Feinberg, 75B. THE STOCK MARKET: © David Davidson, 30; © Globus Brothers, 142B; © Roy Morsch, 50; © Chris Springman, 206; © Bill Wasserman, 80. THE STOCK SHOP: © Mike Yamashita, 20. © MARTHA SWOPE PHOTOGRAPHY: 81, 92–3, 94, 95, 96TR,BL, 97. © JOE VIESTI: 98–9TC, 186L, 186–7C. WHEELER PICTURES: © Kim Steele, 135R. WHITNEY MUSEUM OF AMERICAN ART: Synthetic polymer on canvas, 85½ x 85½ inches; Collection of Whitney Museum of American Art; Purchase with funds from The Friends of the Whitney Museum of American Art; Acq. #63.34, 168LC. WOODFIN CAMP AND ASSOCIATES: © Nathan Beum, 188–9TC; © George Hall, 188–9B. © WOODSTOCK CHIMES ® WOODSTOCK PERCUSSION, INC.: 120.